COMPLETE
Comprehension
FICTION

MW01688347

Jennifer Serravallo

# COMPLETE Comprehension

## FICTION

# Assess

## Collecting Readers' Responses to Chapter Books

HEINEMANN
Portsmouth, NH

**Heinemann**
361 Hanover Street
Portsmouth, NH 03801–3912
*www.heinemann.com*

*Offices and agents throughout the world*

© 2019 by Jennifer Serravallo

All rights reserved. No part of this book may be reproduced in any form or by any electronic or mechanical means, including information storage and retrieval systems, without permission in writing from the publisher, except by a reviewer, who may quote brief passages in a review, and with the exception of reproducibles (identified by the *Complete Comprehension: Fiction* copyright line), which may be photocopied for classroom use.

*Heinemann's authors have devoted their entire careers to developing the unique content in their works, and their written expression is protected by copyright law. We respectfully ask that you do not adapt, reuse, or copy anything on third-party (whether for-profit or not-for-profit) lesson-sharing websites.*
**—Heinemann Publishers**

"Dedicated to Teachers" is a trademark of Greenwood Publishing Group, Inc.

**A Note About Text Levels Assigned to Children's Books**
For the purposes of consistency, all children's books used for assessment in *Complete Comprehension: Fiction* were leveled through www.fountasandpinnellleveledbooks.com. Their leveling system is used by others across other leveling sites and apps, but the website is the only official source for F&P Text Level Gradient™ levels. If you use another leveling source, or rely on a different alphabetic leveling system without an official source, you may find discrepancies across different sites and apps.

The author and publisher wish to thank those who have generously given permission to reprint borrowed material:

Cover image from *The Tiger Rising*. Copyright © 2001 by Kate DiCamillo. Reproduced by permission of the publisher, Candlewick Press, Somerville, MA.

Cover image from *Taking Sides* by Gary Soto. Copyright © 1991 by Gary Soto. Published by HMH Books for Young Readers, an imprint of Houghton Mifflin Harcourt Publishing Company. Reprinted with permission from the publisher.

Cover image from *SeeSaw Girl* by Linda Sue Park, illustrated by Mou-Sien Tseng and Jean Tseng. Copyright © 1999 by Linda Sue Park. Published by Sandpiper, an imprint of Houghton Mifflin Harcourt Publishing Company. Reprinted by permission of the publisher.

Cover image from *Because of Winn-Dixie*. Copyright © 2000 by Kate DiCamillo. Reproduced by permission of the publisher, Candlewick Press, Somerville, MA.

Cover image from *One Tiny Turtle*. Text copyright © 2001 by Nicola Davies. Illustrations copyright © 2001 by Jane Chapman. Reproduced by permission of Candlewick Press, Somerville, MA, on behalf of Walker Books Ltd., London.

**Library of Congress Cataloging-in-Publication Data**
Names: Serravallo, Jennifer, author.
Title: Complete comprehension. Fiction / Jennifer Serravallo.
Description: Portsmouth, NH : Heinemann, 2019. | Includes bibliographical references. Contents: v. 1. Assess — v. 2. Evaluate — v. 3. Teach.
Identifiers: LCCN 2018050002 | ISBN 9780325109541 (bundle) | ISBN 9780325109763 (Assess) | ISBN 9780325109770 (Evaluate) | ISBN 9780325109787 (Teach)
Subjects: LCSH: Reading comprehension—Study and teaching (Elementary). | Fiction—Study and teaching (Elementary).
Classification: LCC LB1573.7 .S475 2019 | DDC 372.47—dc23
LC record available at https://lccn.loc.gov/2018050002

*Editors:* Zoë Ryder White and Heather Anderson
*Production:* Hilary Goff
*Cover and interior designs:* Suzanne Heiser
*Photography:* Nicholas Christoff, Michelle Baker, and Sherry Day
*Cover art:* © Maxchered / Getty Images
*Typesetter:* Gina Poirier Design
*Manufacturing:* Steve Bernier and Val Cooper

Printed in the United States of America on acid-free paper
23 22 21 20 19 VP 1 2 3 4 5

# Contents



To access the online resources, visit **http://hein.pub/ccfic-login.** Enter your email address and password (or click "Create New Account" to set up an account). Once you have logged in, enter keycode **WholeBooksF** and click "Register."

# Foreword

Seven years ago, Jennifer Serravallo published her groundbreaking *Independent Reading Assessment*. It's now been revised and reformatted to be an even more effective tool for assessing, evaluating, and teaching whole-book reading. The central reason for the resource remains the same: although elementary school educators have a variety of assessment tools for evaluating oral reading development, they have few tools for evaluating silent reading development across the curriculum, beyond standardized multiple-choice reading assessments. Because those tools are built upon short passages, it's always been a leap of faith to think they tell us much about students' comprehension of longer texts. For far too long, we've needed something more reliable. This is a primary reason everyone should welcome Serravallo's *Complete Comprehension* for Fiction and Nonfiction, and her brand-new companion professional book, *Understanding Texts & Readers: Responsive Comprehension Instruction with Leveled Texts*. And there are other reasons to welcome those new resources.

First, Serravallo has created an assessment system that evaluates children's reading of actual books! That's right, students read real children's literature as they are being assessed.

Second, the assessment focuses on students' understanding of the text. It helps illuminate their fiction-reading skills in key areas: identifying the theme, noting character traits, studying plot structure, understanding figurative language, and more. In other words, it helps us measure the complex ways to understand and appreciate all texts.

Third, the system guides you in developing your expertise as an evaluator while providing you with ideas for how to foster student learning of the literacy skills mentioned previously.

What Serravallo has developed is really the first complete system for monitoring and developing students' comprehension of whole books. Her Assess, Evaluate, and Teach cycle provides you with enough detail to feel comfortable in gathering, interpreting, and using assessment data to craft on-target whole-class, small-group, and individual instruction. The guidelines are written in teacher-friendly language and are very practical and easy to follow.

So here is my advice: Assess one student using the recommended texts. Then, engage in the evaluation to understand the student's comprehension development and find a goal. Finally, implement strategies for fostering growth in that reader. By learning the ropes with a single student, you will see the potential of this assessment tool to document the student's progress and inform your instruction. From that point, administer the assessment to additional students and, in the process, grow your expertise as a literacy teacher.

You may have noticed, as I have, that we're seeing a resurgence of interest in children's literature, robust classroom libraries, and time devoted to independent reading—both at school and at home. *Complete Comprehension* will provide the very sorts of information needed to assist students in developing their understanding of fiction, and to assist you in understanding comprehension so you can support readers as they grow. So, get to it.

**Richard L. Allington**
*Professor Emeritus of Literacy Studies*
*University of Tennessee*

*The Assess, Evaluate, and Teach cycle provides you with enough detail to feel comfortable in gathering, interpreting, and using assessment data to craft on-target whole-class, small-group, and individual instruction.*

# Introduction

Whether you plan to start by assessing your entire class or only a few students, you will find guidance in this section for how and when you might administer the assessment, language to use when talking to students about it, frequently asked questions, and much more. The following introductory pages won't take long to read; spending a few minutes with them will help you get oriented and streamline the process for you going forward.

## Getting Ready to Administer the Assessment: 3 Steps

1. **Lay out your materials.**
   You should have the following: 28 trade books, two titles for each level, J–W

Book-specific sheets containing labels with preprinted prompt numbers and page numbers.

Three professional resources: the *Assess* book you're holding now, the *Evaluate* book containing guidelines and rubrics you'll use to evaluate student responses, and the *Teach* book containing over 100 strategies to use in whole-class, small-group, and one-on-one instruction.

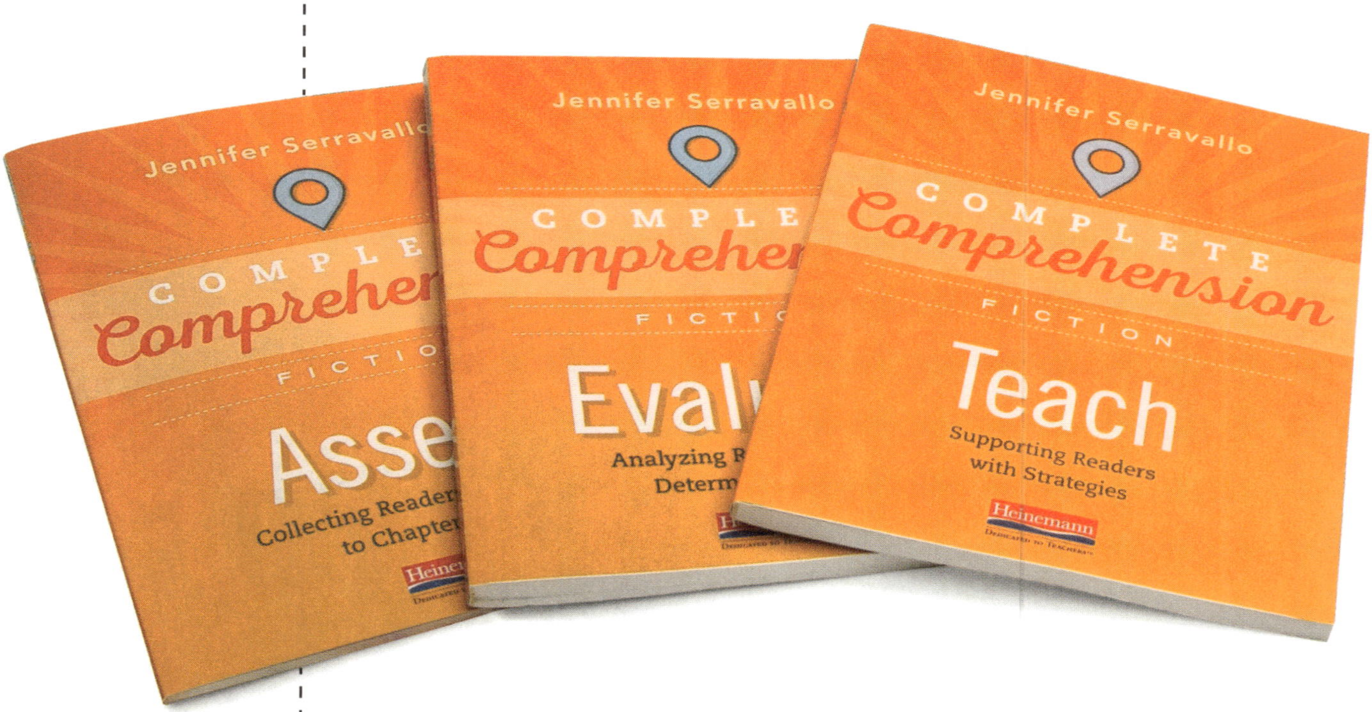

2. **Affix the labels to book pages**, using the book titles on the label sheets and page numbers on the labels themselves as a guide to ensure accuracy. To speed this step along, you may enlist the help of a parent volunteer or classroom aide. These labels stay in the book so you'll only need to affix them once! There is a round sticker for the book's cover and a rectangular sticker for the spine. Affix these stickers so that you and students know to return them to the *Complete Comprehension* box rather than the classroom library.

3. **Print forms.** For every book, there is a unique Response Form (for students) and Planning Form (for teachers). There is also a universal Reading Log (for students) that can be used with any book. Many teachers choose to print out all forms at once and store them in a binder for easy photocopying. Others prefer to print them out as needed. The Response Form and Reading Log will be used first, during the assessment. The Planning Form will be used later, when you are evaluating the student's responses.

To access the online resources, visit **http://hein.pub/ccfic-login.** Enter your email address and password (or click "Create New Account" to set up an account). Once you have logged in, enter keycode **WholeBooksF** and click "Register."

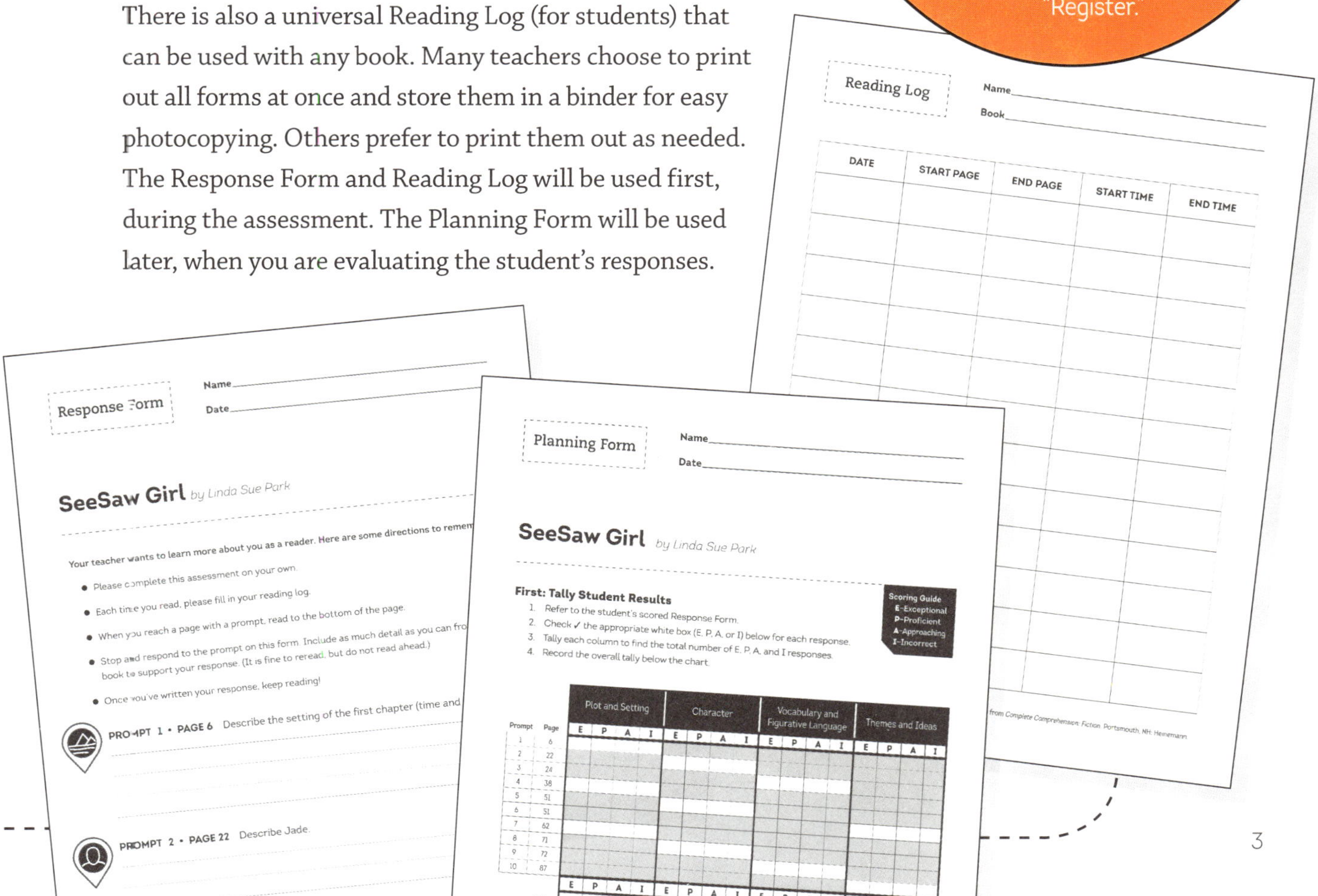

## Administering the Assessment: 5 Steps

1. **Select Students to Assess.** Decide whether you want to assess the entire class or focus on particular students. (See Tips for Deciding When to Assess, page 8, for guidance.)

2. **Gather Your Materials.** Make sure the trade books you'll be offering students have the prompt labels inserted on the correct pages. Make sure you have copies of the Response Forms for each book you plan to use, and enough Reading Logs for each student you plan to assess. You can print them as needed from the Online Resources.

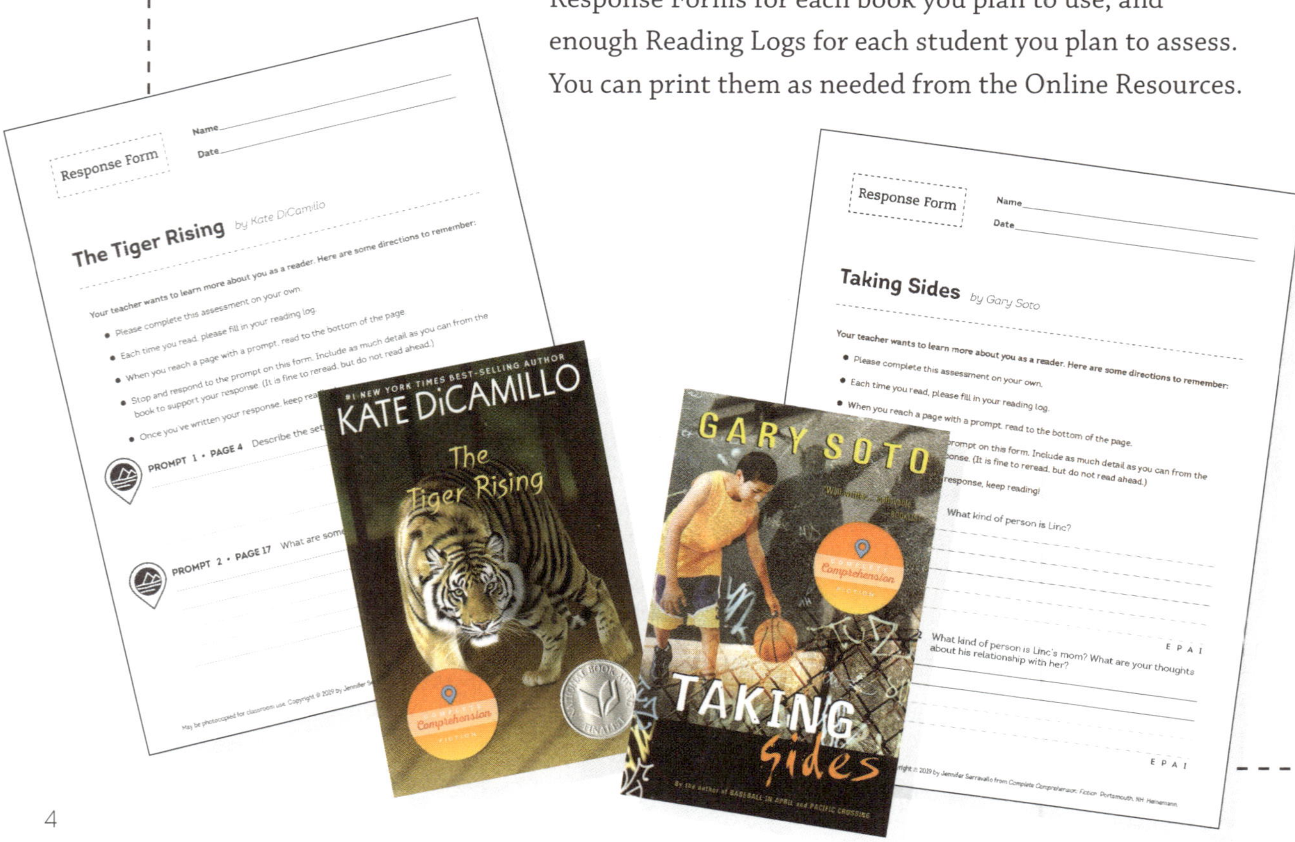

**3. Introduce the Assessment to the Class.** Schedule five to ten minutes during class to meet with the students you'll assess. Tell them what they will do (i.e., read a book and respond to prompts along the way), what you hope to learn about them as readers, and how you will use the information to teach them. (Read more about introducing the assessment on pages 9–10.)

Watch a video of Jen introducing the assessment to a class in the Online Resources.

**4. Help Students Select a Book and Begin the Assessment.** Offer each student a choice of books you believe they will be able to read independently. (See Helping Students Select a Book and Begin on page 10 and Q&As on pages 20–31 for additional advice.) Give students the book they choose, its corresponding Response Form, and a Reading Log.

Watch a video of Jen offering students book choices in the Online Resources.

**5. Allow Enough Time to Read and Respond.** There is no set time limit; allow students as long as necessary to read the book and respond to the prompts on their Response Form, filling in the Reading Log when they start and finish each reading sitting. (Depending on the book's level, length of the book, and how many minutes your students can sustain independent reading each day, the assessment should take somewhere between one hour and several days to complete.)

## What's Next? Evaluate and Teach.

Once a student finishes reading the book and responds to all prompts, return the trade book to the box and evaluate the student's work as soon as you can, using the rubrics in *Evaluate*. When you're finished, you'll be able to determine an appropriate goal for the student.

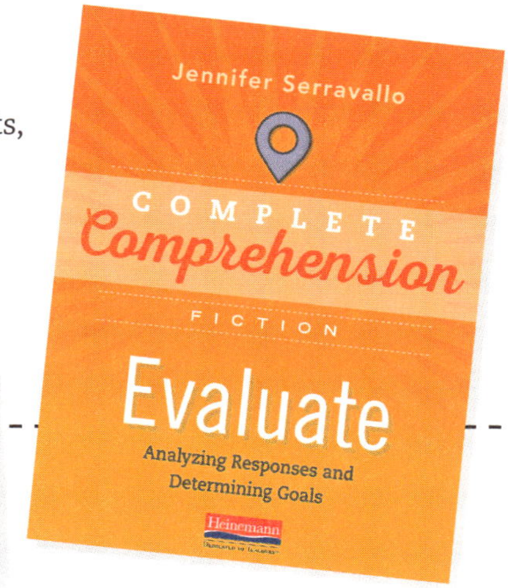


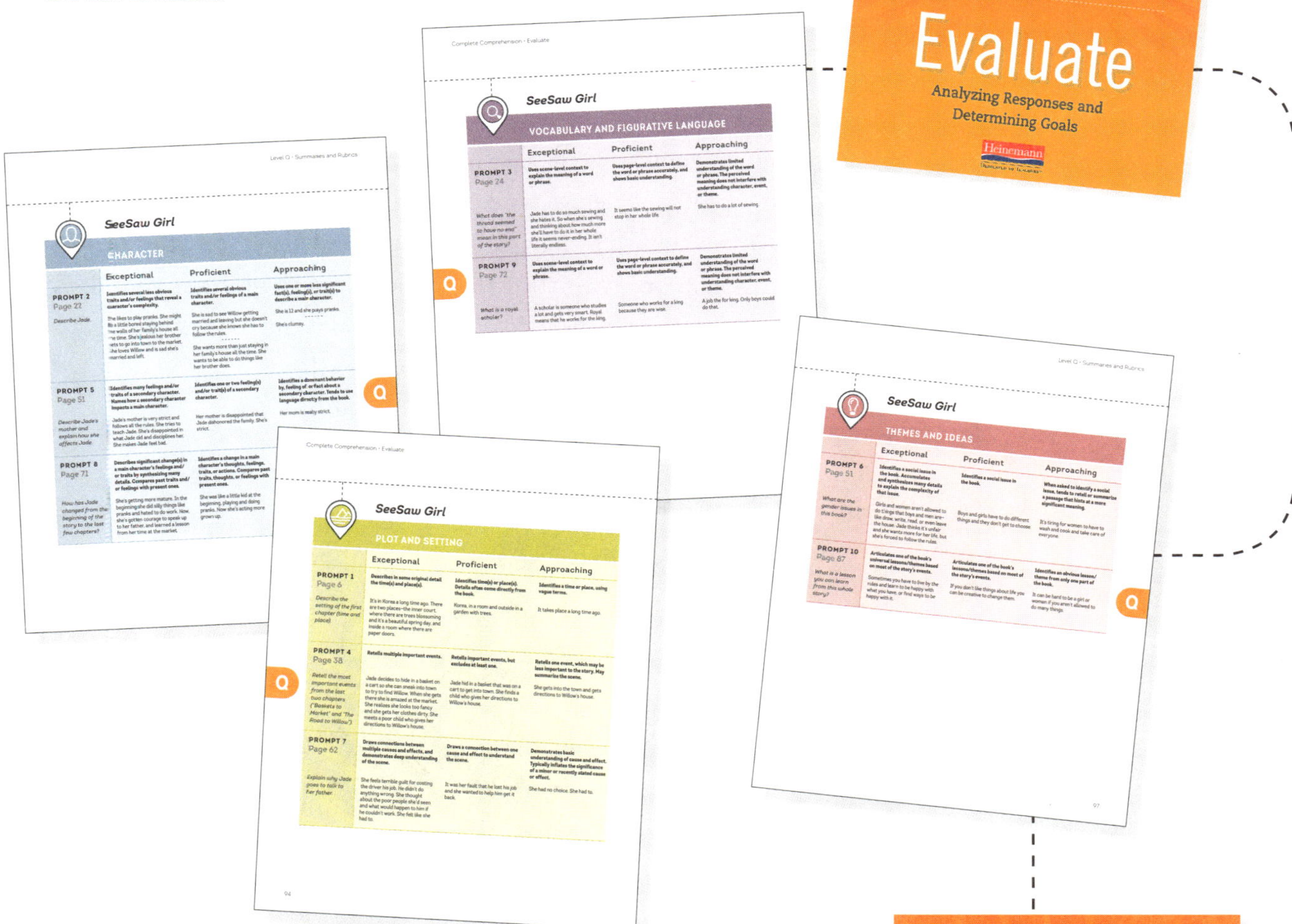


You'll establish the goal with a student in a goal-setting conference and then continue ongoing instruction through whole-class, small-group, and/or individual teaching. You can find over 100 strategies in *Teach* that can be used in any instructional setting.

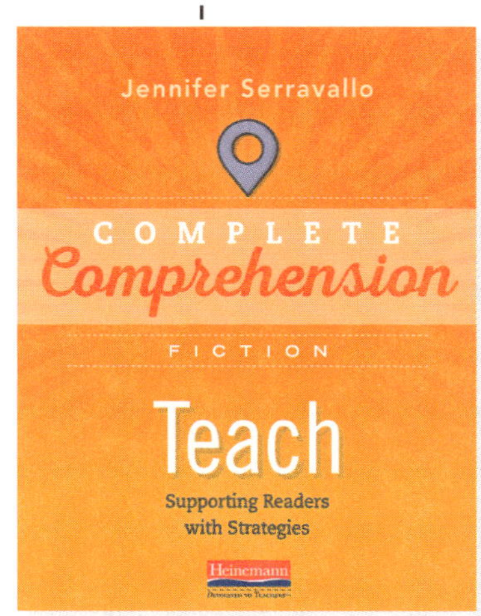

## Tips for Deciding When to Assess

The assessment is designed to be flexible. You can choose to assess your whole class at once, or assess individual students or small groups of students as needed. If you choose to assess the whole class, it often works best to carry out the process over a couple of weeks. For example, you may start with a few students on Monday, a few more on Tuesday, two more on Wednesday, and so on. This allows you to continue conferring or doing small-group instruction with students who are not yet reading the assessment books and to evaluate the Response Forms of those who are soon after they're turned in. If you start everyone on the same day, you'll get a deluge of completed Response Forms at once and may feel overwhelmed by having to evaluate them all soon after receiving them. Staggering their start times allows you to continue your daily routines, and the assessment folds naturally into the flow of your day, so instruction never comes to a complete halt.

**COMMON SCENARIOS FOR USING THE *COMPLETE COMPREHENSION* ASSESSMENT**

| Your Goal | What to Do and When to Do It |
|---|---|
| Gain a class profile to match students to books and to determine student goals. | Assess the entire class over the first couple of weeks of the school year. |
| Discover how students have progressed as readers at midyear. | Assess the entire class over a midyear month, such as January or February. |
| Document progress from the beginning of the year to the end, provide data for next year's teachers, and celebrate students' growth. | In late spring, assess the entire class. Then, in conferences, provide students with tangible feedback that helps them to focus their reading over the summer and beyond. |
| Focus on a few students who you believe are ready to read higher-level texts or who are in need of a new reading goal. | Assess those students on an as-needed basis throughout the year. |
| Determine why a student doesn't seem to be making progress. | Assess the student to confirm their current strengths and needs. Then plan a few conferences over a short period to propel the student forward. |

## Introducing the Assessment to the Class

I recommend introducing the assessment to the whole class at once. Even if you don't plan on assessing every student right now, you may do so over the course of the year, and it will save time in the long run to let all students know what to expect. You will give students further directions when they're about to begin.

Start by showing students a sample trade book prepared with labels and the corresponding Response Form. You might want to use a digital projection system to display a labeled book page and the form to make sure everyone can see them.

After giving students an overview, always ask them to turn to a partner and repeat what you told them. That way, you can confirm that they understand what to do. Following the turn-and-talk, don't be surprised if students come up with questions you didn't anticipate or details you may not have covered.

## Points to Make When Introducing the Assessment

- "This is not a 'test,' and there is nothing to 'pass.'"
- "I am trying to learn what you think about as you read, so please complete the form just the way I ask you to."
- "This assessment is one of many things we'll do together as readers this year. It helps me know what books to recommend to you, and what goals to focus on to help you grow as readers."
- "Responding to the prompts is a lot like talking in literature discussions. In literature discussions, we talk about characters, and what happens in the story, and why it happens. With this assessment, you think on paper about those same things."
- "Please read in a quiet place where you can do your best work." (It's up to you to decide whether to allow students to take the book between home and school.)
- "Do not ask anyone to help you with the assessment, because the purpose is to learn about you as a reader. If you don't understand a prompt, reread it and try your best. If you just can't think of a way to respond to it, write 'I don't understand' and keep reading."
- "Each time you read, please note in your Reading Log the date, what time you started reading and what time you stopped, and your start and end pages. If you are still learning to tell time, use a digital clock, like the one on a grown-up's cell phone or the microwave or cable box in your home. This will give me important information about how you pace yourself when you read so that I can help you if necessary. When you've finished your book completely, it's no longer necessary for you to log your time and pages. If you haven't filled in all the lines in your Reading Log, it's OK." (If your students aren't familiar with logging their reading, you may want to go into more detail here, providing a sample and/or model.)

- "When you read the book, you'll come across orange labels. When you see a label, read the page on which it appears. Then stop, read the prompt on the Response Form, and respond to it on your Response Form. When responding to the prompt, think about everything you've read up to that point. If you'd like to reread, you may. Do not read ahead until you've responded to the prompt."
- "Respond to every prompt as completely as you can. You don't need to write complete sentences—words and phrases are fine—but use as much supporting detail as you can. For example, if the prompt asks, 'What kind of person is Mary?' a good complete response would be as follows: 'Kind. Thoughtful. Caring. A good sister. She's helpful to everyone around her.' An incomplete response wouldn't contain supporting detail: 'Nice.' So write quickly—just make sure your ideas are clear, detailed, and readable—and get back to reading!"
- "After reading the book, you will have a chance to share what you thought about it, and to reflect."

## Helping Students Select a Book and Begin

When you're ready to assess students, gather them into small groups based on the books that you believe they will be able to read independently, and with comprehension. (See the next section for tips on which books to offer as choices.) Once each student has chosen a book, hand out the corresponding Response Forms (printed from the Online Resources). You can offer some brief guidance for responding to prompts, but remember, this assessment is meant to help you understand what students can do independently, so you should only offer assistance in understanding procedures involved with the task and not offer more prompts to help them comprehend the book or respond to the prompt. Doing so will give you a false sense of what students comprehend when reading independently.

## Tips for Determining What Books to Offer as Choices

If you are using this assessment tool at the start of the year, you may be able to rely on information from each student's previous teacher for a sense of where to begin. However, if the student didn't read at all over the summer, they may need a lower-level text than what they were reading at the end of the previous year.

If the previous teacher cannot provide that information, you may choose to administer a quick assessment, such as a running record, to get a sense of the level at which a student can read a short passage with fluency, accuracy, and comprehension. This can get you in the ballpark.

Alternatively, you may choose to give a student a short passage (perhaps a photocopy of a chapter from a leveled book) that you suspect is close to the level at which the student can read independently. You can ask a student to read a passage, give a retelling, and answer a few inferential questions about it. Or, in conferences, you can ask questions about the most recent book a student says they have read independently to determine whether that student comprehended it.

None of the previous suggestions is as precise as the *Complete Comprehension* assessment. So just hang in there and be comfortable with some trial and error to determine the right texts for each student. Once a student has selected a book, you may find it helpful to peek at their Reading Log and responses to the first few prompts on the Response Form to get a sense of whether the chosen book is a good match. If you're noticing a very slow reading rate and/or several incorrect responses, you can allow the student to choose another book that may be a better fit.

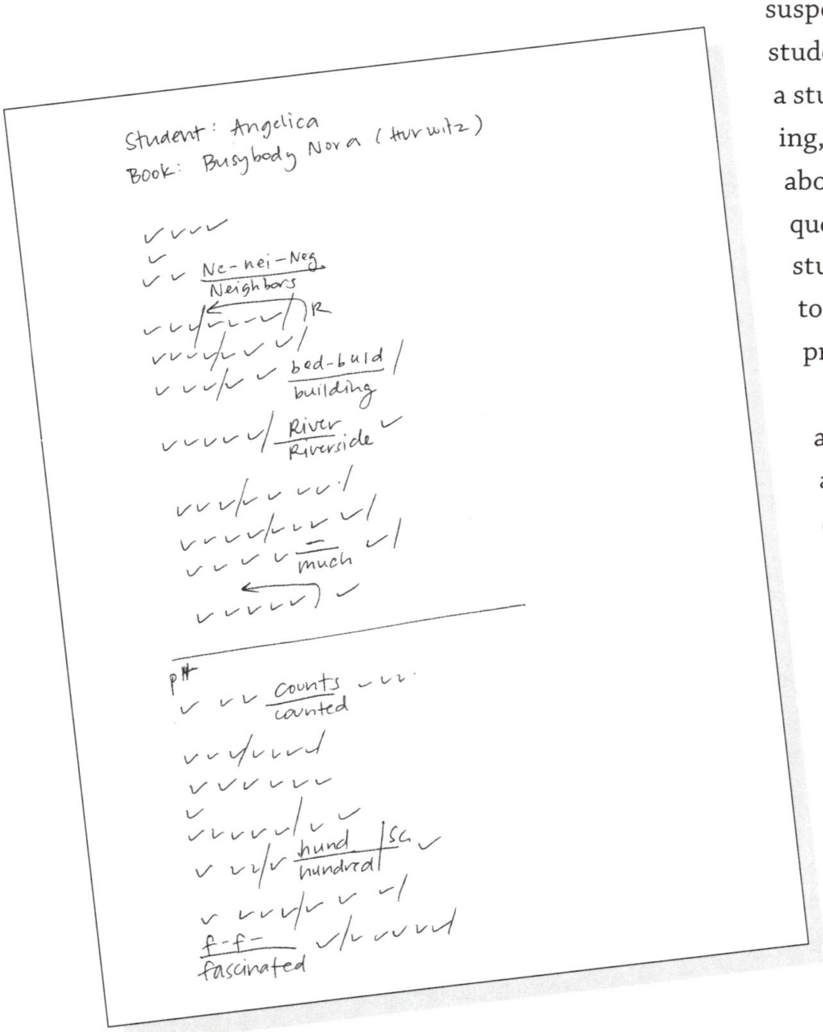


Running Record

## Tips for Introducing the Book Choices

Introduce the assessment book choices by bringing together a small group of children to show and tell them about the books that you feel they will be able to read with comprehension. You might just tell them a bit about each book based on the back-cover blurb or general information about the book. Just make sure you don't give away any information that the students may use when responding to prompts on the Response Form. In a nutshell, present the books enthusiastically—and highlight what makes each one interesting.

For example, you might say, "The books you'll choose from are *Andy Shane and the Very Bossy Dolores Starbuckle* and *Days with Frog and Toad*. Both are chapter books. *Andy Shane* is about a kid about your age who faces some problems in school. And this *Frog and Toad* book has all animal characters, and each chapter features a different adventure or problem. Think about the kinds of books you like to read. Take a look at them. Which book looks more interesting to you?"

An important note: I do not put the book's level anywhere on the book, nor do I talk to students about the book's level when they are making their selections. Knowledge of the level is a tool I use, but not one that I want children concerned about when selecting between a book.

If you have more than one student who wants to read the same book, you will need to stagger the start of their assessments. Record each student's book choice and give out the available books to start. As the first student finishes, it will free up the copy for the next student who wanted to read that book. Remember, I don't advise starting the assessment with the majority of students on the same day, because you will get too many Response Forms back all at once and, as a result, you won't be able to evaluate students and have goal-setting conferences with them in a timely fashion.

## What to Expect: Sample Completed Response Form

To give you a picture of what you might expect from students, I want to show you a form completed by Sondra, who read Linda Su Parks's *See Saw Girl*, and explain what stands out to me. In *Evaluate*, I provide detailed guidance on analyzing your students' completed forms, using book-specific rubrics.

Sondra filled out the Reading Log each time she read. Her teacher had Sondra do all her reading in school, during independent reading time. (You could allow your students to read in school and/or at home, as long as you are sure they will be able to concentrate on the book without anyone at home interfering.)

Each prompt on the Response Forms starts with the prompt number and book page number on which the prompt appears, so students can easily refer to the text in the midst of writing responses.

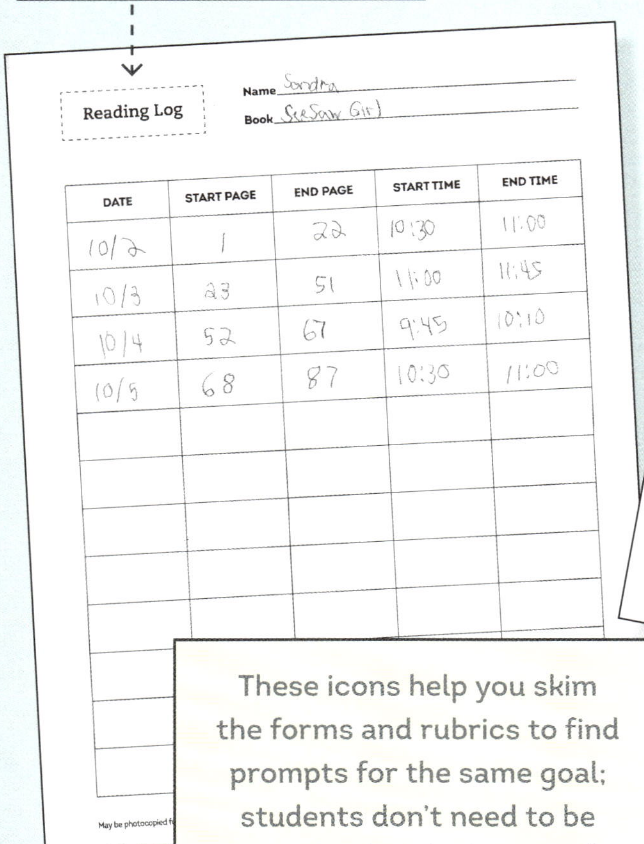

Reading Log

Name Sondra

Book SeeSaw Girl

| DATE | START PAGE | END PAGE | START TIME | END TIME |
|---|---|---|---|---|
| 10/2 | 1 | 22 | 10:30 | 11:00 |
| 10/3 | 23 | 51 | 11:00 | 11:45 |
| 10/4 | 52 | 67 | 9:45 | 10:10 |
| 10/5 | 68 | 87 | 10:30 | 11:00 |

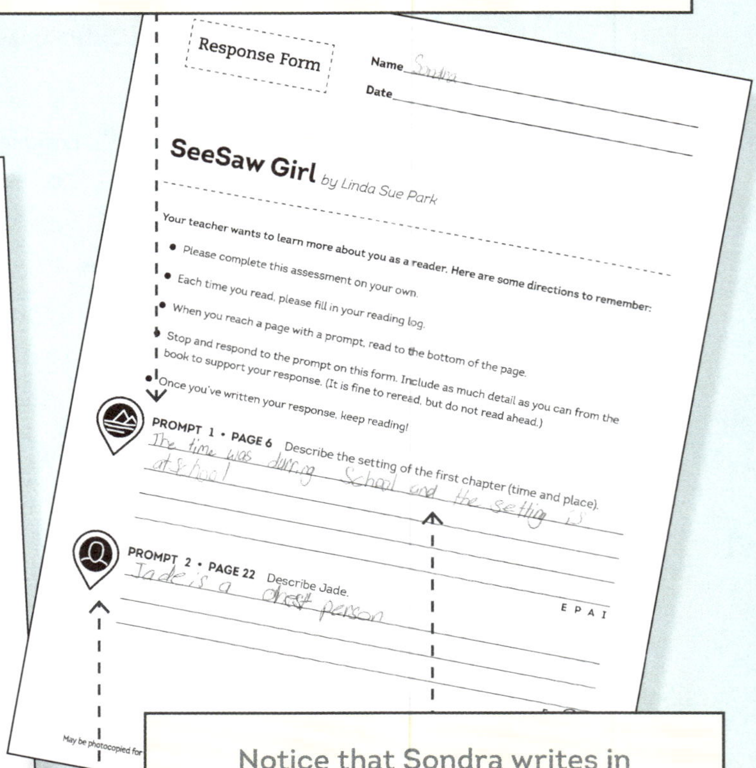

Response Form

Name Sondra

Date

**SeeSaw Girl** by Linda Sue Park

Your teacher wants to learn more about you as a reader. Here are some directions to remember:

- Please complete this assessment on your own.
- Each time you read, please fill in your reading log.
- When you reach a page with a prompt, read to the bottom of the page.
- Stop and respond to the prompt on this form. Include as much detail as you can from the book to support your response. (It is fine to reread, but do not read ahead.)
- Once you've written your response, keep reading!

PROMPT 1 • PAGE 6 Describe the setting of the first chapter (time and place).

The time was during School and the setting is at school

PROMPT 2 • PAGE 22 Describe Jade.

Jade is a great person

E P A I

These icons help you skim the forms and rubrics to find prompts for the same goal; students don't need to be concerned with them at all.

Notice that Sondra writes in complete sentences. This isn't necessary. If students choose words and phrases, that's OK, too, as long as they provide enough detail to give you a window into their thinking.

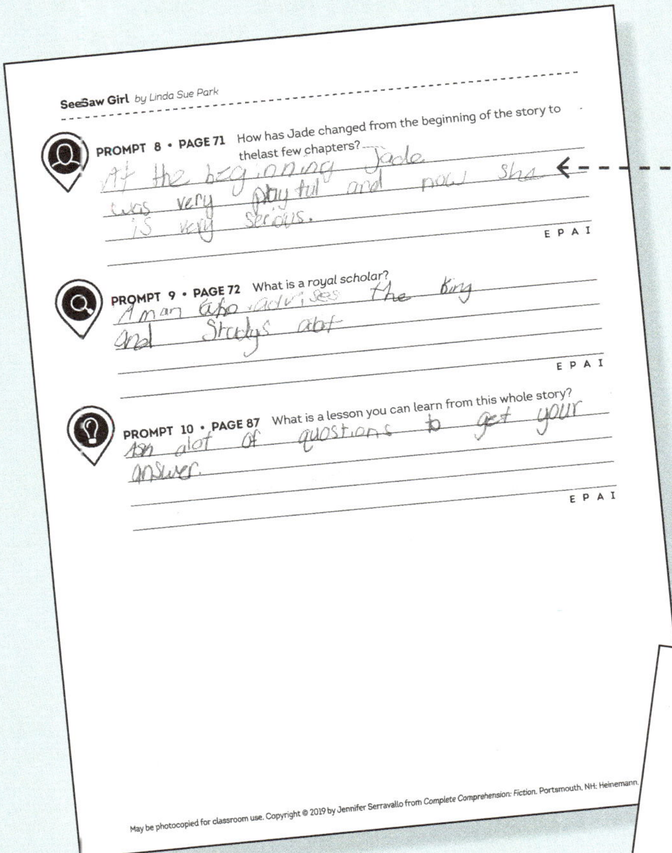

SeeSaw Girl *by Linda Sue Park*

PROMPT 8 • PAGE 71 How has Jade changed from the beginning of the story to thelast few chapters?

At the beginning Jade was very playful and now she is very serious.

E P A I

PROMPT 9 • PAGE 72 What is a *royal scholar*?

A man who advises the king and studys abt

E P A I

PROMPT 10 • PAGE 87 What is a lesson you can learn from this whole story?

ask alot of questions to get your answer.

E P A I

May be photocopied for classroom use. Copyright © 2019 by Jennifer Serravallo from *Complete Comprehension: Fiction*. Portsmouth, NH: Heinemann.

Notice that even on the last page, Sondra's responses are as complete as they are on the first page. This is a good indicator of her stamina.

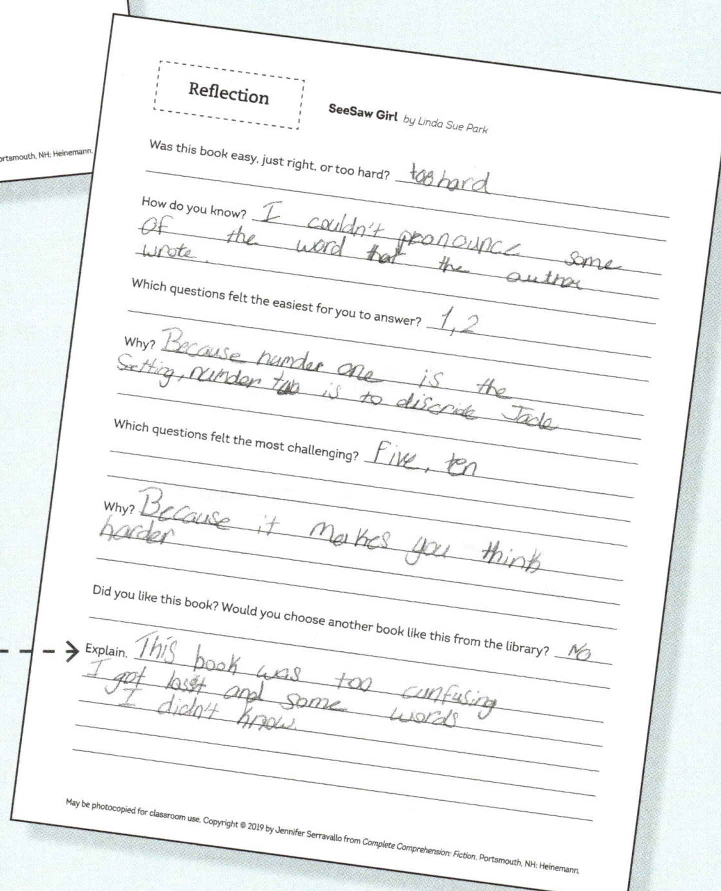

Reflection

SeeSaw Girl *by Linda Sue Park*

Was this book easy, just right, or too hard? too hard

How do you know? I couldn't pronounce some of the word that the author wrote.

Which questions felt the easiest for you to answer? 1, 2

Why? Because number one is the setting, number two is to discribe Jade

Which questions felt the most challenging? Five, ten

Why? Because it makes you think harder

Did you like this book? Would you choose another book like this from the library? No

Explain. This book was too confusing I got lost and some words I didn't know.

May be photocopied for classroom use. Copyright © 2019 by Jennifer Serravallo from *Complete Comprehension: Fiction*. Portsmouth, NH: Heinemann.

Be sure students complete this Reflection section because it helps you know how well they are able to monitor comprehension, and may give you inspiration in matching each child to other books. The questions about which prompts were easier and more challenging can be an important jumping off point for your goal-setting conference (see *Teach* 14–15).

## Finding a Good Pace: When Are Students Ready to Read More Challenging Texts?

Teachers who have used this assessment often ask me, "When do I know to reassess students to see if they are ready to read more challenging books?" Although there is no magic number of days or weeks, there are ways to make that decision wisely and thoughtfully. The sections that follow—guiding principles, a reflection checklist, grade-level benchmarks, and a suggested assessment timetable—will help you.

### Guiding Principles

1. **Focus on a student's goal.** This assessment is designed to help you become an expert observer of students and to help you determine an area (or areas) of focus for your instruction with them. Specifically, once a student has taken the assessment, you will decide on a goal (or goals): Reading Engagement, Plot and Setting, Character, Vocabulary and Figurative Language, or Themes and Ideas. That goal will help you select lesson ideas from *Teach,* know what to look for when working with students, and help you provide targeted feedback to students.

2. **Look for true independence.** When students have developed independence meeting the goal—meaning they demonstrate proficiency with the goal-related skills without any prompting or support—you may decide it's time to reassess. Avoid waiting for the entire class to be "ready." Instead, reassess students on a rolling basis, as individual students develop independence with their goal(s).

3. **Go for depth, not speed.** Don't feel rushed to move a student to more complex books; instead, you and the student should savor their comprehension and engagement in the books they are reading now. Focus your energy on working with students to develop "proficient" and "exceptional" comprehension in all four goal categories before moving them ahead. (For a discussion

of proficiency levels, see page 9 of *Evaluate*.) Deepening their comprehension across the board in books they are currently reading gives students a strong foundation for moving on to more challenging books. When they encounter more complex elements in books at the next level, they will be well prepared.

## A Checklist for Reflecting on Readers' Rate of Growth

The amount of time a student reads books at and around a given level before they are ready to be assessed with a more challenging text depends on a variety of factors. If you aren't sure whether it's time to reassess, here are some things to ask yourself:

- How much time does the student spend reading in school each day? Is it enough?
- How much time does the student spend reading at home? Is it enough?
- Does the student read on the weekends? Vacations?
- Is the student engaged during independent reading time?
- Does the student know how to select just-right books?
- Does the student seem engaged during whole-group, small-group, and individual instruction?
- Does the instruction the student receives match the student's goal?
- Is the student an emergent bilingual?
- Does the student have any learning differences?

## Grade-Level Benchmarks

As discussed in depth in *Understanding Texts & Readers*, text leveling is not a perfect science, a wide variety of variables impact a student's ability to read a text with comprehension, and it's not possible to "level a reader" (Serravallo 2018). Therefore, it is important to note that this assessment is not meant to be used to assign a student to one level or limit students' choices of books (nor should any assessment!). Instead, it is meant to offer more information to a teacher who wishes to offer responsive comprehension instruction, and to allow a teacher to compare a student's whole-book comprehension against other comprehension assessments that may already be in use to make thoughtful plans for the student's reading instruction.

Despite the myriad factors that impact students' rate of reading growth and what text will be a good match at any given time (see *Understanding Texts & Readers* pages 15–24) we can look at grade-level benchmarks for a *general* sense of the *approximate* number of levels a reader is expected to progress through within a year (Serravallo 2018). Follow the links to two grade-by-grade benchmark charts that are used widely in schools. Note that Teachers College Reading and Writing Project's chart lists *independent levels* while Fountas and Pinnell's chart lists *instructional levels*. You will notice different benchmark levels on each in several instances.

- Teachers College Reading and Writing Project Level Benchmarks: http://connect.readingandwritingproject.org/file/download?google_drive_document_id=17U_HBm4NIzJzc5bs8wzjwA7E6zvkkihP

- Fountas and Pinnell's "Instructional Level Expectations" Chart: http://literacycollaborative.org/blog/adjustments-in-text-level-expectations/

No matter which chart you end up using, one of these or another, such as one provided by your district, it is crucially important to remember that all students progress at different rates, that text variables (length, topic, format, genre) mean all books at one level aren't exactly the same, and that reader variables (interest, prior knowledge, stamina) mean that a reader is likely to be able to read a range of texts with comprehension at any given time.

## A Suggested Timetable for Reassessing Readers

Here's a rough estimate of when you may find students are ready to be reassessed. It's important to regularly confer with students to check on how they are progressing with their goal(s); that is the best way to know when students are ready to be reassessed. Notice the time span for reassessment is shorter in lower levels and longer in higher levels. Remember that every reader is different and readiness for more challenging texts is not fixed.

| If a student is currently reading texts at and around these levels . . . | Look to see if they are ready to be reassessed after . . . |
|---|---|
| J, K, L | 2-2½ months |
| M, N, O, P, Q | 2½-3½ months |
| R, S, T | 3-4 months |
| U, V, W | 3½-4½ months |

## Q&A: Frequently Asked Questions About Administering the Assessment

I've collected and provided answers to the following questions from teachers who have used this assessment. Skim all the questions and answers now, and return to this section as your own questions arise.

### Q. *Why does this assessment cover Levels J–W, and not A–Z?*

A. Level J is the first level at which students are unlikely to read a whole book during a running record or an online assessment. It is also the level at which many students have strong print and fluency skills, and running records begin to offer less help for the teacher who wants to know what to focus on for instruction. This is not true for all students—some students reading books at Level O, P, or Q may need support with print and fluency skills and should be assessed with a running record—but it is true for many students. A whole-book assessment like this one is meant to look at how students track character development across an entire story, synthesize multiple plot events, track changes in settings from chapter to chapter, infer themes and ideas based on the whole story, and so on—skills that cannot be assessed in shorter texts. It helps teachers notice how students reading book-length fiction texts handle these challenges, and allows teachers to track students' progress throughout fourteen text levels and across several grade levels.

*Complete Comprehension* ends at Level W because students who can read Level W texts—students who have received proper and complete instruction around comprehension skills and strategies—should be able to read flexibly at higher levels, often beyond Level W. This resource helps track their progress throughout elementary school and into middle school benchmark levels (though some students will be reading at those levels into later middle school and even high school).

### Q. *How do I fit this into my schedule? Do I assess everyone at once or a few students at a time?*

A. It's up to you. Some teachers take a break in between units to create a few assessment windows throughout the year. For example, if you're just wrapping up a unit, you can take a couple of weeks to do this assessment (which, of course, involves lots of independent reading), before moving into the next unit. This will give you periodic up-to-date assessment information to share with parents at parent-teacher conferences or to use on report cards. Assessing a few times a year provides this up-to-date information.

Alternatively, you can assess students on a rolling basis as needed. You might decide to assess students when they are new to reading books at a certain level to determine goals as they read books at and around the new level. Or you might decide to assess a child who seems stuck at a level for a while to figure out what's holding that student back. (See Tips for Deciding When to Assess, page 8.)

You can use this assessment as many times as you like. It is even possible to assess students with both books at the same level if that information would be helpful for planning your instruction.

## Q. *How long will it take to administer the assessment?*

A. The first time you introduce the assessment, it'll take about five minutes to orient your class to what it is and what's expected. (See Introducing the Assessment to the Class, page 9.) When you introduce the book choices, expect to spend an additional five minutes per group. (See Helping Students Select a Book and Begin, page 11.)

Depending on the level and length of books the students choose and the number of minutes your class can sustain independent reading each day, the assessment should take *students*—not you—somewhere between one hour and several days to complete. While some students in your class are reading the assessment books and completing the Response Forms, you can continue providing small-group or individualized instruction to children who are not engaged in reading an assessment book.

Once your students are experienced with the assessment, it shouldn't take any more of your instructional time. Students will be able to read the books and respond to prompts on their own. Your greatest time commitment will be devoted to analyzing student responses and planning your instruction based on what you find, as explained in *Evaluate*. Analyzing responses will probably take about ten to fifteen minutes per student at first, but less time as you become familiar with the assessment, the books, and the rubrics in *Evaluate*.

## Q. *At what point should I use this assessment—when students first read books at and around a new level or when they have been reading books at and around a level for a while?*

A. Using the assessment at either of these points could be beneficial. When a student is ready to read more challenging texts (meaning they have shown strong comprehension within all goals at the previous level and/or have shown the ability to read a text with fluency, accuracy, and comprehension when reading for a running record), you're likely looking for some new ideas for what to teach. When you aren't getting enough information about comprehension from your current reading assessments, or when a child seems stuck, this assessment could help you pinpoint what skills to focus on so you know what area of comprehension could be strengthened.

## Q. *What leveling system was used to determine the levels of the twenty-eight books in this resource?*

A. I chose to rely on the qualitative leveling framework called the F&P Text Level Gradient™ (Fountas and Pinnell 2016). To determine a book's level, each is evaluated by trained experts who study the text using ten characteristics: genre, text structure, content, themes and ideas, language and literary features, sentence complexity, vocabulary, illustrations, and book and print features.

For the purpose of consistency, all books in this resource were leveled through www.fountasandpinnellleveledbooks.com. Their leveling system is used by others across other leveling sites and apps, but that website is the only official source. If you use another leveling source, or rely on a different alphabetic leveling system without an official source, you may find discrepancies.

## Q. *What if more than one of my students wants to read the same book? Do you have tips for administering this assessment?*

A. Record each student's choices, and allow one student to begin. As the desired book becomes available, give it to the next student on the list. This is a good option if your goal is to assess many or all students during a particular assessment window.

Another option is to acquire more copies of the books and print the labels that go inside from the online resources (or mark the pages with sticky notes or other labels you have on hand). If you choose to do this, be sure to acquire paperback editions of the books with the same ISBNs as those that came with your kit so that the page numbers for the prompts match; other publishers' editions may not have a one-to-one prompt-to-content match. Just be aware that it's not advised to have many students reading assessment books at the same time as there won't be anyone left for you to teach.

## Q. *How do I determine the level of book to give a student to start?*

A. Ideally you will offer students books that are close to the level you think is appropriate for them when they read independently. Perhaps you've taken running records to get a sense of where each student reads a short text comfortably, with fluency, accuracy, and comprehension. If it is the beginning of the year, you may have information from each student's prior teacher, which will help you choose a starting level.

If you're still uncertain, you might schedule a one-on-one conference in which you ask a student to read aloud a passage from a self-selected independent reading book; then you could ask a few comprehension questions about the passage. The book is probably a good choice if the child reads at least 97 out of 100 words correctly, with fluency, and provides evidence of literal and inferential comprehension.

When a student begins an assessment, you can always take a glance at the Response Form as they work through the first few prompts, checking to see that the responses make sense. If the child seems to be laboring through the book or is disengaged or confused, stop the assessment early and have him or her switch to a book at a lower level.

## Q. *What if the student chooses a book that they have already read independently or heard read aloud?*

A. In my research I've found that whether the book is new to students or not, their responses to the prompts in this assessment reveal valuable information about their comprehension across the board. Therefore, it is likely that even if a student has already read the book independently, or a teacher has read it aloud, you'll still get a lot of valuable information from the assessment.

That said, going forward, it would be good practice to choose alternate books to read aloud to students and reserve the *Complete Comprehension* titles for assessment purposes only.

## Q. *What if the assessment books are already in my classroom library?*

A. You may choose to remove them to limit access prior to the assessment. As the year progresses and you're confident that you no longer need them for assessment purposes, you can reinstate them. Another option is to turn those classroom library copies into extra assessment copies, as long as those library copies are the same edition (with the same ISBN) as the ones included in the kit. If they're not, the page numbers on which students need to stop and respond may be off.

## Q. *Does it matter which of the two books a student picks? Will I get the same information from both?*

A. As discussed in *Understanding Texts & Readers*, leveling books is not a perfect science (Serravallo 2018). There are differences between both assessment books at almost every level. Some books tend to be more plot driven, and others are more character driven.

Some books contain a lot of challenging vocabulary and figurative language, and others at the same level are challenging mostly because of their themes and ideas.

So I encourage you to allow students to choose without worrying too much about the differences between them. The student should choose a book because it is the one they will most enjoy.

### Q. *The overall number of prompts and the number of prompts within each goal vary from book to book. Why is that?*

**A.** The authors of the authentic children's books in this resource did not have assessment in mind when they wrote. Books that are considered to be the same level vary for a number of reasons. Some books are determined to be a certain level based on their challenging vocabulary, whereas others are because of character complexity. So although it would have been tidier to create the same number and types of prompts for every book, it would not have been true to the authors' storytelling and unique style—and would not have taken into account how those variables can affect comprehension.

As a result, books that depend a lot on the reader's ability to monitor for meaning and understand vocabulary, such as Scieszka's *The Time Warp Trio*, have more prompts in the Vocabulary and Figurative Language strand. Books that are rich in symbolism, such as DiCamillo's *Because of Winn-Dixie*, have a higher-than-average number of prompts in the Themes and Ideas strand. Because I felt it was important for the assessment to contain books that would appeal to different types of readers, I chose texts for some levels that were shorter than average for the level (e.g., *Sadako and the Thousand Paper Cranes*) or longer (e.g., *Judy Moody Saves the World!*).

## SAMPLE PROMPTS

***The Time Warp Trio: Knights of the Kitchen Table***

VOCABULARY AND FIGURATIVE LANGUAGE

**Prompt 2, Page 17:** What does "The helmet rang like a thousand church bells" mean?

**Prompt 5, Page 25:** When Sam whispers, "Another great idea from the mind of Sir Fred," what does he mean?

**Prompt 7, Page 33:** What does "make haste" mean in this part?

***Because of Winn-Dixie***

THEMES AND IDEAS

**Prompt 8, Page 109:** Think about this moment. What is Opal learning about life?

**Prompt 10, Page 132:** What do the lozenges and the events of this chapter teach Opal about everyone's life?

**Prompt 12, Page 182:** What lesson or lessons has Opal learned?

## Q. *What if a student starts reading the book only to tell me they don't like it? Should I make the student finish it, or should I offer the student a new choice?*

A. Use your judgment, but in general, I would say allow the student to abandon the book and note the point at which they did so. The student's point of frustration or boredom, and the responses they have given so far on the Response Form, may offer you insights into the kinds of books they like or the kinds of challenges they don't enjoy as a reader.

My philosophy is that children should read books they find enjoyable and interesting that foster a high level of engagement. Since this assessment is meant to offer a window into what readers naturally do when they read independently, it's best if they're reading a book they like.

## Q. *How much help can I provide students when they're taking this assessment?*

A. For this to be a valid assessment of what children can do independently, you need to refrain from offering too much assistance. On the other hand, you don't want students to become frustrated or to hit a stumbling block that they're unable to overcome. I advise you to assist them as little as possible—just enough to keep them moving forward and working through the assessment on their own. For more information on working with students during the assessment, see Helping Students Select a Book and Begin, page 11.

In the development of the assessment, I tried my best to ensure that the prompts are worded to be understood by most children reading a given level of text; I kept the vocabulary and syntax of the prompts in line with the sorts of syntax they'd be expected to encounter in a book at that level. Nonetheless, there may be an instance where a child does not understand what's being asked of them. Although you should refrain from helping the child make sense of the book, it's OK to tell a student the meaning of words—such as *affect*, *emerging*, *theme*, or *significance*—that will help them to understand the prompts, so that the assessment is helping you understand more about their comprehension of the book, rather than whether they understand the prompt

itself. Later, you can review the challenging academic vocabulary from the prompts since they will no doubt encounter them again and again throughout their school experience.

Notice how much persistence and perseverance children have in responding to the prompts, especially those that challenge them. If a student is unable to move forward, it tells you something about them as a reader. When students have difficulty reading, do they usually just plow ahead? What strategies do they have for monitoring comprehension and for fixing misunderstandings? I recommend planning instruction around anything you notice that would support their growth as readers.

All that said, if you notice a student is coming to you for help a lot while reading a book, you may decide to have them try an easier book to avoid creating negative associations with this assessment. Bottom line: An independent reading book is supposed to be enjoyable and understandable. If a child is struggling, it's a signal that the book is too challenging.

## Q. *How complete do the responses need to be?*

A. You can tell from the rubrics and sample student responses in *Evaluate* that an "exceptional" response varies by level in terms of the amount of writing. You may want to take a peek at the rubrics in *Evaluate* to get a sense for this. Usually, a child needs to write more than a word or phrase to demonstrate strong comprehension. Be aware, though, that sometimes a student uses many words in a response, yet says nothing of substance, and therefore likely warrants an "approaching" score. Don't tell students to "write a lot." Instead, tell them to write as much as they need to respond to the prompt completely. The writing spaces on the Response Form are compact, to encourage quick, but substantive, jotting. It's important that the reader writes quickly and gets back to reading.

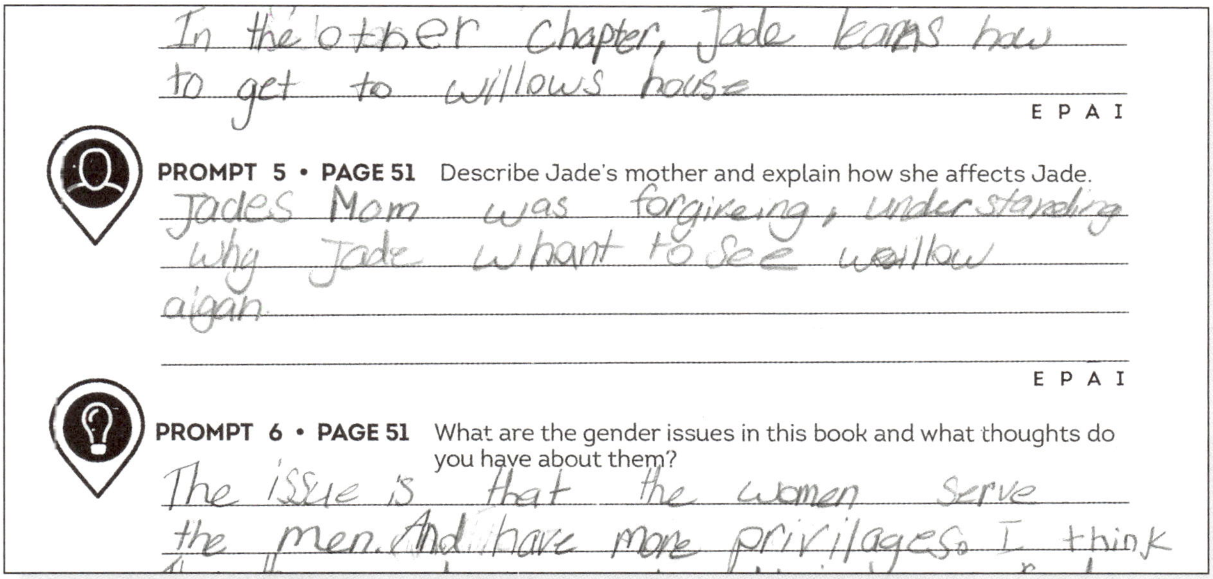
In the other chapter, Jade learns how to get to willows house

E P A I

PROMPT 5 • PAGE 51 Describe Jade's mother and explain how she affects Jade.

Jades Mom was forgiveing, understanding why Jade whant to see wallow agian

E P A I

PROMPT 6 • PAGE 51 What are the gender issues in this book and what thoughts do you have about them?

The issue is that the women serve the men. And have more privilages. I think

## Q. *Could responses be given orally instead of in writing?*

A. Sure. However, the assessment is designed to require a bare minimum of instructional time and teacher involvement, to allow the teacher to continue working with other students while one or some take an assessment. If a student has an assistant, such as a paraprofessional who works alongside them on a regular basis, it is fine for that person to scribe the student's responses as they speak them, as long as no help with content or rewording of the child's response is provided. If the child wants to dictate responses into an app, use speech-to-text software on a laptop or tablet, or use a handheld digital recorder, that, too, is fine.

Be sure the student is responding to the prompts *during reading*. That is, when the student encounters a prompt in the book, they should read to the end of that page, and then stop and respond to the prompt. Any modification to the assessment that allows children to record their responses in a way that accurately represents their thinking is fine, as long as this procedure is kept in mind.

***Q. Some of the students I work with are emergent bilinguals. What accommodations do you recommend?***

A. The aim of this assessment is to help teachers evaluate student comprehension of whole texts, so it's important to make the accommodations necessary to get the best read on your students' understanding as possible.

For some students who speak two or more languages, receptive and productive language abilities may not be completely in sync. In other words, some students will be able to read and comprehend texts with more depth than they are able to express orally or in writing in English. Many bilingual education scholars and researchers have suggested that children be encouraged to use

their strengths and their full linguistic repertoire during formative assessments; this means they would respond in whatever language they feel most comfortable in, or in a combination of languages (Ascenzi-Moreno 2018; Abedi, Hofstetter, and Lord 2004). Think of it this way—one question type in this assessment asks students to describe characters. An emergent bilingual student may be able to read about and understand the character, and to think deeply about the kind of person the character is, but when it comes to writing about it, they might not have the English vocabulary necessary to give a complete response. Instead of writing that the character is "generous" and "thoughtful" a student might just write "nice" because it is a word they know in English, even if they do have a more nuanced understanding of the character. By forcing students to respond only in English, we miss an opportunity to learn about their thinking, and this may skew the results. If they write their answer in the language they are most comfortable with, we can then see that they are doing the thinking work required of that prompt, that they have the skills they need to infer about the character, but that they need support with vocabulary for character traits in English.

If you choose to allow students to respond in a language other than English, or in a combination of English and another language, you could use Google Translate or other software to translate the student's work before moving on to evaluate their responses.

## Q. *Can I use this assessment in place of running records?*

A. The teachers across the country who piloted this assessment have remarked that they liked to replace running records with this assessment once children begin reading books at and around Level J, or that they use both running records and this assessment for Levels J and K, and then transition into only this assessment for Level L and beyond except in cases where the running record would provide helpful information (i.e. students who are still working on print and fluency skills). They found that a whole-book assessment offered a more complete picture of the reader than a short-passage assessment.

### Q. *Is this the only tool I should use to assess my students' reading?*

A. I would advise against making finite conclusions about student performance based on the results of only one assessment tool. Reading comprehension is complicated and nuanced, and the more sources of information you have from which to glean teaching ideas, the better. Once you know what you want to teach, watch the child and follow up; look at what they are doing in independent reading, monitor how the data you got from this assessment matches and/or departs from standardized test results, listen carefully to responses during lessons, and so on. Confer, conduct small groups, drop in on conversations, collect and read reading notebooks, and read what students write in the margins of their books and on sticky notes. Ongoing, continuous assessment and tweaking of your teaching are the best ways to meet the needs of each of your students.

### Q. *When might I use this assessment a second time with a student?*

A. Once a student has completed the assessment and you've evaluated the responses, you'll have a conference during which you establish a goal together. Through a mixture of whole-class, small-group, and individual lessons, you'll coach the student as they work on the goal over time.

Working toward a goal may last weeks or more than a month, depending on the levels of text the student is reading, the length of time they have been reading books at and around a certain level, and how much time the student devotes to accomplishing the goal. Once the student has demonstrated strong understanding within all four goals, is engaged with reading, and can adequately write about reading, reassess them. This time, assess them at a higher level; assuming the student can read the text independently with comprehension, the assessment should help you to identify a new goal. See Tips for Deciding When to Assess, page 8, and Finding a Good Pace, page 16, for details on when to assess and consider reassessing.

## Q. I have both *Complete Comprehension: Fiction* and *Complete Comprehension: Nonfiction*. How do you recommend I balance administering both?

A. I would alternate using the *Fiction* and *Nonfiction* resources. Use these assessments to inform instruction in an upcoming unit of study. For example, if in September you plan to teach a character study, then begin the year with *Fiction*. Before you move to a nonfiction-focused unit such as Informational Book Clubs in October/November, give students a *Nonfiction* assessment to help craft your unit goals and individualized plans for each reader.

# Prompts at a Glance

On the following pages, you'll find first an example of an entire Response Form and Reading Log (to be used by students). Each book has a unique Response Form available in the Online Resources. The samples on pages 35–37 will help you get a sense for layout and length. Please remember to download any forms you may need before offering students a choice of what book to read.

The page spreads that follow offer you, for quick reference, a level-by-level, book-by-book view of all prompts, organized by goal, appearing in each unique Response Form.

Icons next to each prompt will help you scan and find all the prompts of the same type when it's time for evaluating responses, the next step. Students don't need to know what the icons stand for, but feel free to tell them if they are curious!

Print out book-specific Response Forms like this one, and a universal Reading Log, from the Online Resources.

Response Form

Name__________

Date__________

## Taking Sides *by Gary Soto*

**Your teacher wants to learn more about you as a reader. Here are**

- Please complete this assessment on your own.
- Each time you read, please fill in your Reading Log.
- When you reach a page with a prompt, read to the bottom
- Stop and respond to the prompt on this form. Include as m book to support your response. (It is fine to reread, but do
- Once you've written your response, keep reading!

**PROMPT 1 • PAGE 10** What kind of person is Lin

**PROMPT 2 • PAGE 32** What kind of person is Linc's mom about his relationship with her?

E P A I

May be photocopied for classroom use. Copyright © 2019 by Jennifer Serravallo from *Complete Comprehension: Fiction.* Portsmouth, NH: Heinemann.

**Taking Sides** *by Gary Soto*

**PROMPT 3 • PAGE 41** What is the "field work" mentioned here, and why is it important to Linc and Monica?

E P A I

**PROMPT 4 • PAGE 42** What does "The basketball filled with air and went bumping down the stairs, out of control" mean?

E P A I

**PROMPT 5 • PAGE 49** What kind of person is Tony? Why is he important to Linc?

E P A I

**PROMPT 6 • PAGE 51** Describe where Linc lives now and where he used to live.

E P A I

May be photocopied for classroom use. Copyright © 2019 by Jennifer Serravallo from *Complete Comprehension: Fiction.* Portsmouth, NH: Heinemann.

**Taking Sides** *by Gary Soto*

**PROMPT 7 • PAGE 62** Why does Linc leave the thrift store and walk to his old school?

E P A I

**PROMPT 8 • PAGE 86** In what ways are issues about race coming up?

E P A I

**PROMPT 9 • PAGE 99** What does the word "carnal" mean in the sentence, "...Tony was no longer his *carnal*"?

E P A I

**PROMPT 10 • PAGE 106** What are some conflicts Linc is experiencing?

E P A I

May be photocopied for classroom use. Copyright © 2019 by Jennifer Serravallo from *Complete Comprehension: Fiction*. Portsmouth, NH: Heinemann.

Students will encounter prompts that go with each question type in a different order in each book. Sometimes Plot is first, other times Character. They are reading examples of authentic children's literature, and what the book calls for differs from book to book. On the pages that follow, you'll get an overview of all the prompts for each book, organized by goal for easy access.

The number of lines provided should be enough to respond to the prompt adequately and completely. If they need more space, feel free to encourage children to continue onto the back of their paper or onto a separate piece of paper. Stress to children that longer isn't necessarily better, but they do need to respond to each prompt thoughtfully and completely.

**Reflection** — **Taking Sides** *by Gary Soto*

Was this book easy, just right, or too hard? ____________

How do you know? ____________

Which questions felt the easiest for you to answer? ____________

Why? ____________

Which questions felt the most challenging? ____________

Why? ____________

Did you like this book? Would you choose another book ...

Explain. ____________

May be photocopied for classroom use. Copyright © 2019 by Jen...

Encourage students to reflect on the assessment experience. This reflection can be a jumping-off point for your goal-setting conference (view a sample goal-setting conference in the Online Resources), can give you a sense of students' ability to monitor their own comprehension, and can help you to recommend books to them in the future.

**Reading Log**

Name ____________

Book ____________

| DATE | START PAGE | END PAGE | START TIME | END TIME |
|---|---|---|---|---|
| | | | | |
| | | | | |
| | | | | |
| | | | | |
| | | | | |
| | | | | |
| | | | | |
| | | | | |
| | | | | |
| | | | | |
| | | | | |
| | | | | |

...classroom use. Copyright © 2019 by Jennifer Serravallo from *Complete Comprehension: Fiction*. Portsmouth, NH: Heinemann.

Ask students to log their reading each time they sit to read the assessment book. Their reading rate is one piece of the comprehension picture. You'll download one Reading Log from the Online Resources that can be copied to use with any of the assessment books.

level J

# *Zelda and Ivy: The Runaways*

by Laura McGee Kvasnosky

## PLOT AND SETTING

**Prompt 2, Page 15:** Retell this chapter, "The Runaways."

**Prompt 6, Page 35:** What problem is Zelda having?

## CHARACTER

**Prompt 1, Page 5:** Describe the kind of character Zelda is.

**Prompt 4, Page 22:** What is Ivy feeling in this story?

## VOCABULARY AND FIGURATIVE LANGUAGE

**Prompt 5, Page 31:** What is a *concoction*?

**Prompt 7, Page 42:** What is *creative juice*?

## THEMES AND IDEAS

**Prompt 3, Page 15:** What is a lesson the sisters learn?

**Prompt 8, Page 42:** What lesson did Zelda learn in this story?

level J

# *Poppleton in Winter*

by Cynthia Rylant

## PLOT AND SETTING

**Prompt 1, Page 11:** What problems is Poppleton having?

**Prompt 6, Page 34:** Why did Cherry Sue go to Poppleton's house?

**Prompt 8, Page 42:** What problems is Poppleton having?

## CHARACTER

**Prompt 2, Page 15:** How is Poppleton feeling?

**Prompt 7, Page 35:** What kind of character is Cherry Sue?

**Prompt 9, Page 43:** How have Poppleton's feelings changed?

## VOCABULARY AND FIGURATIVE LANGUAGE

**Prompt 3, Page 15:** What is a *picket fence*?

**Prompt 5, Page 29:** What does the word *molding* mean in this story?

## THEMES AND IDEAS

**Prompt 4, Page 17:** What did Poppleton learn in this story?

**Prompt 10, Page 48:** What can you learn from this story?

level **K**

# *Andy Shane and the Very Bossy Dolores Starbuckle*

by Jennifer Richard Jacobson

## PLOT AND SETTING

**Prompt 3, Page 14:** What are some problems that Andy is having?

**Prompt 5, Page 35:** How is Andy's problem getting worse?

**Prompt 6, Page 40:** Why does Granny start singing and dancing?

## CHARACTER

**Prompt 1, Page 7:** What kind of person is Dolores?

**Prompt 2, Page 10:** What kind of person is Andy Shane?

**Prompt 8, Page 51:** How is Andy acting differently from before?

## VOCABULARY AND FIGURATIVE LANGUAGE

**Prompt 4, Page 24:** What is the "Granny Webb Stare"?

**Prompt 7, Page 45:** In this part, what does "Dolores Starbuckle's face turned the color of a fire ant" mean?

## THEMES AND IDEAS

**Prompt 9, Page 56:** What is a lesson Andy learns by the end of the story?

**Prompt 10, Page 56:** What is a lesson Dolores learns by the end of the story?

level K

# *Days with Frog and Toad*

by Arnold Lobel

## PLOT AND SETTING

**Prompt 6, Page 41:** Retell what happens in this chapter.

**Prompt 7, Page 51:** What happens to make Toad's hat fit him?

**Prompt 8, Page 59:** What's the problem in this story?

## CHARACTER

**Prompt 1, Page 7:** What kind of character is Toad?

**Prompt 5, Page 27:** What kind of character is Frog?

## VOCABULARY AND FIGURATIVE LANGUAGE

**Prompt 2, Page 9:** What does "down in the dumps" mean in this part?

**Prompt 4, Page 22:** What does Toad mean when he says, "This kite is a joke"?

## THEMES AND IDEAS

**Prompt 3, Page 15:** What lesson does Toad learn about life?

**Prompt 9, Page 64:** What lesson does Toad learn in this story?

level L

# *Cam Jansen: The Mystery of the Stolen Diamonds*

by David A. Adler

## PLOT AND SETTING

**Prompt 2, Page 9:** Retell what has happened so far.

**Prompt 4, Page 30:** List all the things Cam is doing to try to figure out who stole the diamonds.

**Prompt 8, Page 45:** Explain how Cam figured out who stole the diamonds.

## CHARACTER

**Prompt 1, Page 7:** What kind of person is Cam?

**Prompt 3, Page 14:** What kind of person is Eric?

**Prompt 9, Page 50:** What new ideas do you have about the kind of person Cam is?

## VOCABULARY AND FIGURATIVE LANGUAGE

**Prompt 6, Page 34:** What does *innocent man* mean in this part?

**Prompt 7, Page 38:** What does the word *thief* mean in this part?

**Prompt 11, Page 58:** What does *nice couple* mean in this part?

## THEMES AND IDEAS

**Prompt 5, Page 30:** What lesson are you learning about solving a mystery?

**Prompt 10, Page 54:** What is a lesson you've learned from this story?

level **L**

# *Pinky and Rex and the Bully*

by James Howe

## PLOT AND SETTING

**Prompt 3, Page 12:** Explain what Pinky's problems are.

**Prompt 4, Page 17:** Retell the most important events of Chapter 3.

## CHARACTER

**Prompt 5, Page 23:** Explain how Pinky is feeling.

**Prompt 7, Page 37:** How have Pinky's feelings changed from the beginning of the story to now?

## VOCABULARY AND FIGURATIVE LANGUAGE

**Prompt 1, Page 2:** Explain what *sissy* means.

**Prompt 2, Page 10:** Explain what *paint* means on this page.

## THEMES AND IDEAS

**Prompt 6, Page 33:** What is a lesson that Pinky's learning from Mrs. Morgan?

**Prompt 8, Page 40:** What lesson can you learn about life from this story?

level **M**

# *Judy Moody Saves the World!*

by Megan McDonald

## PLOT AND SETTING

**Prompt 2, Page 14:** Explain why Judy Moody is in a mood.

**Prompt 5, Page 41:** Retell the three or four most important events from the whole story so far.

**Prompt 8, Page 77:** Why is Stink mad at Judy?

## CHARACTER

**Prompt 1, Page 10:** What kind of person is Judy Moody?

**Prompt 9, Page 106:** Explain how Judy feels in this chapter.

**Prompt 10, Page 121:** How is Judy changing?

level M

# *Judy Moody Saves the World!*

by Megan McDonald

## VOCABULARY AND FIGURATIVE LANGUAGE

**Prompt 3, Page 22:** What does Judy mean when she says, "Rare!"?

**Prompt 4, Page 32:** Why does Stink call Judy "batty"?

**Prompt 7, Page 67:** What does "Judy had ants in her pants" mean?

## THEMES AND IDEAS

**Prompt 6, Page 43:** What is a lesson you've learned about saving the world?

**Prompt 11, Page 144:** What lesson does Judy learn by the end of the story?

level **M**

# *Stuart Goes to School*

by Sara Pennypacker

## PLOT AND SETTING

**Prompt 4, Page 19:** Why does Stuart work so hard to bring in something special for "Our Big Interesting World"?

**Prompt 6, Page 36:** Tell all the ways Stuart has used the hole from his pocket so far.

**Prompt 9, Page 50:** What problems does Stuart's drawing cause?

## CHARACTER

**Prompt 1, Page 5:** What kind of person is Stuart?

**Prompt 7, Page 40:** How is Stuart feeling?

level **M**

# *Stuart Goes to School*

by Sara Pennypacker

## VOCABULARY AND FIGURATIVE LANGUAGE

**Prompt 2, Page 13:** What does "his ears begin to blow up" mean in this part?

**Prompt 5, Page 21:** Explain the ways the word *hole* is being used in this part.

**Prompt 8, Page 42:** What does Mrs. Spindles mean when she says, "Stop pulling my leg!"?

## THEMES AND IDEAS

**Prompt 3, Page 16:** What is a lesson Stuart has learned so far?

**Prompt 10, Page 56:** What is a lesson Stuart learns by the end of the story?

level **N**

# *Amber Brown Is Not a Crayon*

by Paula Danziger

## PLOT AND SETTING

**Prompt 4, Page 30:** Retell the ways that Amber shows she doesn't want Mrs. Bradley to like the house.

**Prompt 5, Page 37:** List the kinds of things Amber and Justin do together as friends.

**Prompt 7, Page 61:** What's the problem with Justin and Amber's friendship right now?

## CHARACTER

**Prompt 2, Page 13:** What kind of person is Amber?

**Prompt 6, Page 53:** What ideas do you have about Justin?

**Prompt 9, Page 71:** What kind of person is Amber Brown's mom?

level N

# *Amber Brown Is Not a Crayon*

by Paula Danziger

## VOCABULARY AND FIGURATIVE LANGUAGE

**Prompt 1, Page 9:** In the sentence "Every time we start studying a new country, we 'fly' there," what does *fly* mean?

**Prompt 8, Page 63:** What does the word *obnoxious* mean in this part?

## THEMES AND IDEAS

**Prompt 3, Page 30:** What is a lesson you're learning about friendship from this book?

**Prompt 10, Page 80:** What is a lesson you learned from this book?

level **N**

# *Be a Perfect Person in Just Three Days!*

by Stephen Manes

## PLOT AND SETTING

**Prompt 1, Page 11:** Retell what's happened so far. Why are there headings that say "Chapter One," "Chapter Two," and "Chapter Three"?

**Prompt 6, Page 27:** Why is Milo lying to his friends, teachers, and family?

**Prompt 9, Page 52:** Retell what has happened over the last four pages (pages 49–52).

## CHARACTER

**Prompt 3, Page 15:** What kind of person is Dr. Silverfish?

**Prompt 4, Page 19:** What kind of person is Milo?

**Prompt 8, Page 46:** What kind of person is Milo's father?

level N

# *Be a Perfect Person in Just Three Days!*

by Stephen Manes

## VOCABULARY AND FIGURATIVE LANGUAGE

**Prompt 5, Page 21:** What does "His family would never overlook a lump that size in a million years" mean in this part?

**Prompt 7, Page 31:** What does the phrase "and he just couldn't stomach it" mean in this part?

## THEMES AND IDEAS

**Prompt 2, Page 11:** What is a lesson you're learning so far?

**Prompt 10, Page 58:** What did you learn about life from reading this story?

level O

# *Jake Drake, Bully Buster*

by Andrew Clements

## PLOT AND SETTING

**Prompt 1, Page 12:** Describe the settings (time[s] and place[s]) of Chapters 1 and 2.

**Prompt 3, Page 24:** What is causing Jake to bully his sister?

**Prompt 8, Page 65:** Why does Jake say that Link made the whole thing?

## CHARACTER

**Prompt 2, Page 22:** What kind of person is Link?

**Prompt 6, Page 50:** How has Jake changed?

## VOCABULARY AND FIGURATIVE LANGUAGE

**Prompt 4, Page 26:** What does Jake mean when he says, "I had caught BULLYITIS"?

**Prompt 5, Page 37:** What does the word *might* mean in this part?

## THEMES AND IDEAS

**Prompt 7, Page 60:** What are you learning in this part about the issue of bullying?

**Prompt 9, Page 67:** What is a message or lesson you learned from this book?

level **O**

# *Sable*

by Karen Hesse

## PLOT AND SETTING

**Prompt 2, Page 26:** Retell the most important events in Chapter 3.

**Prompt 7, Page 68:** Think of the whole story so far. What problems is Tate dealing with?

## CHARACTER

**Prompt 4, Page 42:** Describe Mam.

**Prompt 5, Page 49:** Explain how Tate is feeling at this moment in the story.

**Prompt 8, Page 73:** Describe Pap.

## VOCABULARY AND FIGURATIVE LANGUAGE

**Prompt 1, Page 5:** Explain what "there's no trusting a stray" means.

**Prompt 3, Page 30:** Explain what "after I'd wound myself tighter than a rope swing" means.

## THEMES AND IDEAS

**Prompt 6, Page 55:** What is one lesson that you're learning at this part of the story?

**Prompt 9, Page 81:** What lesson can you learn after reading this whole story?

level **P**

# *Almost Zero: A Dyamonde Daniel Book*

by Nikki Grimes

## PLOT AND SETTING

**Prompt 4, Page 42:** What problems is Dyamonde experiencing?

**Prompt 6, Page 61:** Why did Dyamonde's mom let her have her clothes back?

## CHARACTER

**Prompt 3, Page 28:** Explain how Dyamonde is feeling.

**Prompt 5, Page 42:** Describe Dyamonde's mom, Mrs. Daniel.

**Prompt 7, Page 86:** Describe Dyamonde.

## VOCABULARY AND FIGURATIVE LANGUAGE

**Prompt 1, Page 8:** What does "her mom's voice was scary-soft" mean?

**Prompt 8, Page 107:** What does Damaris mean when she says, "There's love in those boxes?"

## THEMES AND IDEAS

**Prompt 2, Page 21:** What is a lesson you're learning so far in this story?

**Prompt 9, Page 112:** What's another lesson you learned from this story?

level P

# *The Time Warp Trio: Knights of the Kitchen Table*

by Jon Scieszka

## PLOT AND SETTING

**Prompt 1, Page 6:** Describe the setting of this scene. Give details.

**Prompt 4, Page 23:** Why are the knights taking the three boys to King Arthur?

**Prompt 9, Page 42:** Explain why King Arthur is so pleased now.

## CHARACTER

**Prompt 6, Page 30:** What kind of person is Merlin?

**Prompt 8, Page 36:** What kind of person is Sam?

## VOCABULARY AND FIGURATIVE LANGUAGE

**Prompt 2, Page 17:** What does "The helmet rang like a thousand church bells" mean?

**Prompt 5, Page 25:** When Sam whispers, "Another great idea from the mind of Sir Fred," what does he mean?

**Prompt 7, Page 33:** What does "make haste" mean in this part?

## THEMES AND IDEAS

**Prompt 3, Page 19:** What is a lesson you've learned from the story so far?

**Prompt 10, Page 42:** What is a lesson you learned from this story?

level **Q**

## *SeeSaw Girl*

by Linda Sue Park

### PLOT AND SETTING

**Prompt 1, Page 6:** Describe the setting of the first chapter (time and place).

**Prompt 4, Page 38:** Retell the most important events from the last two chapters ("Baskets to Market" and "The Road to Willow").

**Prompt 7, Page 62:** Explain why Jade goes to talk to her father.

### CHARACTER

**Prompt 2, Page 22:** Describe Jade.

**Prompt 5, Page 51:** Describe Jade's mother and explain how she affects Jade.

**Prompt 8, Page 71:** How has Jade changed from the beginning of the story to the last few chapters?

level **Q**

# *SeeSaw Girl*

by Linda Sue Park

## VOCABULARY AND FIGURATIVE LANGUAGE

**Prompt 3, Page 24:** What does "the thread seemed to have no end" mean in this part of the story?

**Prompt 9, Page 72:** What is a *royal scholar*?

## THEMES AND IDEAS

**Prompt 6, Page 51:** What are the gender issues in this book?

**Prompt 10, Page 87:** What is a lesson you can learn from this whole story?

level Q

# *Last Summer with Maizon*

by Jacqueline Woodson

## PLOT AND SETTING

**Prompt 1, Page 12:** What problems is Margaret dealing with?

**Prompt 5, Page 61:** Think about how Margaret reacts to Maizon's news. Explain why she reacts this way.

## CHARACTER

**Prompt 2, Page 21:** Describe Maizon and the relationship she has with Margaret.

**Prompt 4, Page 53:** Describe Maizon's grandmother and how she affects Margaret and Maizon.

**Prompt 6, Page 66:** Describe Margaret.

level Q

# *Last Summer with Maizon*

by Jacqueline Woodson

## VOCABULARY AND FIGURATIVE LANGUAGE

**Prompt 3, Page 27:** What does it mean when Ms. Dell says, "Gonna learn about strength this summer, Margaret"?

**Prompt 7, Page 89:** What does Mama mean when she says, "Everything will fall into place"?

**Prompt 8, Page 91:** What does Grandma mean when she calls Maizon an "individualist"?

## THEMES AND IDEAS

**Prompt 9, Page 117:** What are you learning about race in this story?

**Prompt 10, Page 117:** What is a life lesson that you learned from reading this story?

level **R**

# *Sadako and the Thousand Paper Cranes*

by Eleanor Coerr

## PLOT AND SETTING

**Prompt 2, Page 20:** Describe the setting (time and place).

**Prompt 5, Page 45:** Explain how the moments with Kenji are important to the story.

## CHARACTER

**Prompt 1, Page 14:** Describe Sadako's family.

**Prompt 3, Page 27:** Describe Sadako.

**Prompt 8, Page 59:** What new ideas do you have about Sadako?

level **R**

# *Sadako and the Thousand Paper Cranes*

by Eleanor Coerr

## VOCABULARY AND FIGURATIVE LANGUAGE

**Prompt 4, Page 32:** What does *leukemia* mean? Use details from this part tc explain.

**Prompt 7, Page 48:** What does *listless* mean in this part?

**Prompt 9, Page 60:** Read the following line and explain what it means in this story: "But it was like trying to stop the rain from falling."

## THEMES AND IDEAS

**Prompt 6, Page 47:** What do the cranes symbolize for Sadako?

**Prompt 10, Page 63:** What lesson or lessons can you learn from Sadako's story?

**Prompt 11, Page 65:** What have you learned about war from this book?

level **R**

# *Because of Winn-Dixie*

by Kate DiCamillo

## PLOT AND SETTING

**Prompt 6, Page 81:** What do you picture, based on the description on pages 79–81?

**Prompt 7, Page 91:** What are Opal's problems?

**Prompt 11, Page 168:** Why is this moment between Opal and her father important?

## CHARACTER

**Prompt 1, Page 25:** What kind of person is Opal?

**Prompt 4, Page 71:** What kind of person is Gloria Dump? Why is she important to Opal?

**Prompt 5, Page 78:** How are you seeing the preacher in a new way?

level **R**

# *Because of Winn-Dixie*

by Kate DiCamillo

## VOCABULARY AND FIGURATIVE LANGUAGE

**Prompt 2, Page 25:** What does Opal mean when she says, "I could see him thinking about pulling his head back into his shell"?

**Prompt 3, Page 68:** Explain what Opal means when she says, "I could feel her listening with all her heart."

**Prompt 9, Page 115:** What does it mean to "taste" sorrow?

## THEMES AND IDEAS

**Prompt 8, Page 109:** Think about this moment. What is Opal learning about life?

**Prompt 10, Page 132:** What do the lozenges and the events of this chapter teach Opal about everyone's life?

**Prompt 12, Page 182:** What lesson or lessons has Opal learned?

level S

# *The Great Gilly Hopkins*

by Katherine Paterson

## PLOT AND SETTING

**Prompt 4, Page 49:** Why does Gilly say, "I'm coming, Courtney"? Use details from the last couple of pages to explain what's happening.

**Prompt 6, Page 86:** What problems does Gilly experience in this part?

**Prompt 9, Page 137:** What is Gilly realizing in this scene when she thinks, "Oh, my god"?

## CHARACTER

**Prompt 5, Page 68:** What kind of person is Gilly?

**Prompt 7, Page 112:** What kind of person is Mrs. Trotter, and how does she affect Gilly?

**Prompt 10, Page 147:** How is Gilly changing?

level **S**

# *The Great Gilly Hopkins*

by Katherine Paterson

## VOCABULARY AND FIGURATIVE LANGUAGE

**Prompt 1, Page 11:** Explain what the narrator means by this sentence: "This was not the time to start dissolving like hot Jell-O"?

**Prompt 2, Page 26:** Explain what "Miss Harris's voice was more steel than gold now" means?

**Prompt 8, Page 115:** The narrator says, "Gilly's whole body was engulfed in a great aching." Explain what that means.

## THEMES AND IDEAS

**Prompt 3, Page 30:** What issues about race are coming up so far?

**Prompt 11, Page 178:** What lesson or lessons have you learned from th s book?

*level* **S**

# *Taking Sides*

by Gary Soto

## PLOT AND SETTING

**Prompt 6, Page 51:** Describe where Linc lives now and where he used to live.

**Prompt 7, Page 62:** Why does Linc leave the thrift store and walk to his old school?

**Prompt 10, Page 106:** What are some conflicts Linc is experiencing?

## CHARACTER

**Prompt 1, Page 10:** What kind of person is Linc?

**Prompt 2, Page 32:** What kind of person is Linc's mom? What are your thoughts about his relationship with her?

**Prompt 5, Page 49:** What kind of person is Tony? Why is he important to Linc?

level **S**

# *Taking Sides*
by Gary Soto

## VOCABULARY AND FIGURATIVE LANGUAGE

**Prompt 3, Page 41:** What is the "field work" mentioned here, and why is it important to Linc and Monica?

**Prompt 4, Page 42:** What does "The basketball filled with air and went bumping down the stairs, out of control" mean?

**Prompt 9, Page 99:** What does the word *carnal* mean in the sentence, "Tony was no longer his *carnal*"?

## THEMES AND IDEAS

**Prompt 8, Page 86:** In what ways are issues about race coming up?

**Prompt 11, Page 135:** Think about a theme in this book, and use it to explain the title.

level **T**

# *The Tiger Rising*
by Kate DiCamillo

## PLOT AND SETTING

**Prompt 1, Page 4:** Describe the setting.

**Prompt 2, Page 17:** What are some of the obstacles Rob faces?

## CHARACTER

**Prompt 3, Page 25:** What kind of person is Rob?

**Prompt 5, Page 34:** What kind of person is Rob's father? How does he affect Rob?

**Prompt 10, Page 117:** How has Rob changed from the beginning of the story until now?

level **T**

# *The Tiger Rising*

by Kate DiCamillo

## VOCABULARY AND FIGURATIVE LANGUAGE

**Prompt 6, Page 62:** Explain the meaning of the last sentence on this page: "The word was as sweet as forbidden candy on his tongue."

**Prompt 7, Page 66:** Willie May says, "Who don't . . . Who don't know something in a cage?" What does she *really* mean by that?

**Prompt 8, Page 106:** What does Sistine mean by "We're his emancipators"?

## THEMES AND IDEAS

**Prompt 4, Page 26:** What do you think Rob's rash symbolizes?

**Prompt 9, Page 111:** What do you think the tiger symbolizes?

**Prompt 11, Page 121:** What lessons have you learned from this book?

level **T**

# *Joey Pigza Swallowed the Key*

by Jack Gantos

## PLOT AND SETTING

**Prompt 1, Page 49:** What are some problems Joey is having?

**Prompt 2, Page 50:** Explain why Joey's mother is so upset.

**Prompt 4, Page 71:** Why is this moment with the nurse important?

## CHARACTER

**Prompt 3, Page 66:** Think about what you know about Joey from the book so far. What ideas do you have about him?

**Prompt 7, Page 108:** What kind of person is Joey's mom? How does she affect him?

**Prompt 8, Page 125:** What kind of person is Joey's grandma? How is she affecting him?

level **T**

# *Joey Pigza Swallowed the Key*

by Jack Gantos

## VOCABULARY AND FIGURATIVE LANGUAGE

**Prompt 6, Page 102:** What do you think the counselor means when he says, "It's time we look at the big picture"?

**Prompt 9, Page 143:** Joey says, "I felt like Christmas was just a few days away even though it wasn't." What do you think he means?

**Prompt 10, Page 148:** When Ed says, "You gotta face the hand you're dealt and deal with it," what does he mean?

## THEMES AND IDEAS

**Prompt 5, Page 86:** What does Maria's father think about children with special needs? What do *you* think?

**Prompt 11, Page 154:** What lesson or lessons did you learn from reading this story?

level **U**

## *The Watsons Go to Birmingham—1963*

by Christopher Paul Curtis

### PLOT AND SETTING

**Prompt 7, Page 146:** Why are the mom and dad nervous and upset at this point?

**Prompt 8, Page 168:** Describe the setting. Explain how the change in setting has affected the family.

**Prompt 9, Page 179:** Retell what happens in this chapter.

### CHARACTER

**Prompt 2, Page 31:** What kind of person is Kenny?

**Prompt 3, Page 63:** What kind of person is Byron? How does he impact others?

**Prompt 4, Page 74:** What kind of mother is Momma and how does she impact her children?

**Prompt 11, Page 196:** Explain the change in Kenny since returning home.

level **U**

# *The Watsons Go to Birmingham–1963*

by Christopher Paul Curtis

## VOCABULARY AND FIGURATIVE LANGUAGE

**Prompt 1, Page 2:** What do you think *juvenile delinquent* means in this part?

**Prompt 5, Page 77:** What does *welfare food* mean in this part?

**Prompt 6, Page 113:** What does *cutting up* mean in this part?

## THEMES AND IDEAS

**Prompt 10, Page 186:** What do you think the "Wool Pooh" symbolizes to Kenny?

**Prompt 12, Page 206:** What has Kenny learned from his trip to the South?

**Prompt 13, Page 210:** What ideas about race are raised in this book?

level U

# *Loser*

by Jerry Spinelli

## PLOT AND SETTING

**Prompt 5, Page 100:** What problems is Zinkoff experiencing right now?

**Prompt 9, Page 167:** Describe the setting (middle school) and tell why it's important.

**Prompt 10, Page 180:** Why is this moment important?

## CHARACTER

**Prompt 1, Page 33:** What kind of person is Zinkoff?

**Prompt 3, Page 77:** What kind of person is Zinkoff's father? How is he affecting his son?

**Prompt 7, Page 126:** How is Zinkoff changing?

level **U**

# *Loser*

by Jerry Spinelli

## VOCABULARY AND FIGURATIVE LANGUAGE

**Prompt 2, Page 54:** What does the word *atrocious* mean in this part?

**Prompt 4, Page 94:** Explain the meaning of this quotation: "As with all discoveries, it is the eye and not the object that changes."

**Prompt 8, Page 153:** Explain the meaning of the phrase "scooping the fruit out of his life and dropping it into her lap."

## THEMES AND IDEAS

**Prompt 6, Page 107:** What does this part of the story make you realize about bullying?

**Prompt 11, Page 186:** What might the setting symbolize?

**Prompt 12, Page 218:** What are some themes from this book?

level **V**

# *Becoming Naomi León*

by Pam Muñoz Ryan

## PLOT AND SETTING

**Prompt 5, Page 62:** Why do you think the mother showers Naomi, but not Owen, with gifts?

**Prompt 8, Page 122:** What obstacles is Naomi facing right now?

**Prompt 9, Page 145:** Describe the setting at this point. How is the new place affecting Naomi, Gram, and Owen?

## CHARACTER

**Prompt 1, Page 15:** Describe Naomi and her relationships.

**Prompt 2, Page 25:** Describe Naomi and Owen's mother and explain how she affects them.

**Prompt 3, Page 33:** What kind of person is Gram? How does she affect Naomi and Owen?

**Prompt 7, Page 106:** How do you think Naomi is feeling at this point?

**Prompt 10, Page 157:** What changes have you noticed in Naomi since she arrived in Mexico?

level **V**

# *Becoming Naomi León*

by Pam Muñoz Ryan

## VOCABULARY AND FIGURATIVE LANGUAGE

**Prompt 6, Page 74:** What does the author mean by "a found piece of candy when you didn't even know you were craving something sweet"?

**Prompt 11, Page 161:** The term *self-prophecy* appears on this page and throughout the book. What does it mean?

**Prompt 13, Page 237:** On page 236, Naomi says, "It was as if the stampede crashed through the wall in front of me." What does this mean?

## THEMES AND IDEAS

**Prompt 4, Page 42:** Look back at the titles of these first few chapters. What's symbolic about the animals?

**Prompt 12, Page 226:** Think about the book's title. How has Naomi "become" Naomi León?

**Prompt 14, Page 246:** Why do you think the author made carving things (wood, radishes, soap) such a big part of this story?

level **V**

# *Crash*

by Jerry Spinelli

## PLOT AND SETTING

**Prompt 1, Page 4:** Retell this chapter, including the importance of the word *THEN* on page 2.

**Prompt 9, Page 88:** Make a list of the problems Crash is experiencing up to this point.

**Prompt 13, Page 156:** Why does Crash let Penn win?

## CHARACTER

**Prompt 2, Page 20:** What are your thoughts about Penn and his relationship with Crash?

**Prompt 3, Page 27:** Describe Crash and his relationships.

**Prompt 6, Page 60:** Describe Crash's dad. How is he affecting Crash?

**Prompt 7, Page 78:** What kind of person is Scooter? What effect does he seem to have on Crash?

**Prompt 12, Page 140:** How is Crash changing?

level V

# *Crash*

by Jerry Spinelli

## VOCABULARY AND FIGURATIVE LANGUAGE

**Prompt 5, Page 51:** Explain the line "If laughing was hazardous to your health, I'd be in intensive care right now."

**Prompt 10, Page 113:** Crash says Christmas is like "pizza without pepperoni." What does he mean by that?

**Prompt 11, Page 128:** On page 127 it says, "Now there was a crack of daylight between them, like my shell was coming loose." What does that mean?

## THEMES AND IDEAS

**Prompt 4, Page 48:** What do you notice about the attitudes toward gender presented so far? What are your thoughts?

**Prompt 8, Page 86:** Explain how football symbolizes life for Crash.

**Prompt 14, Page 162:** What lesson or lessons did you learn from this book?

level W

# *Home of the Brave*

by Katherine Applegate

## PLOT AND SETTING

**Prompt 1, Page 19:** What obstacles is Kek encountering?

**Prompt 4, Page 91:** Describe America from Kek's perspective.

**Prompt 9, Page 183:** Explain why Kek reacted as he did to Lou's news of selling the farm.

## CHARACTER

**Prompt 2, Page 48:** Describe Kek and his relationships.

**Prompt 5, Page 101:** What kind of person is Hannah? What are your thoughts about her relationship with Kek?

**Prompt 11, Page 217:** What kind of person is Ganwar? What effect is he having on Kek?

**Prompt 12, Page 242:** Think about Part Four. How has Kek changed?

level W

# *Home of the Brave*

by Katherine Applegate

## VOCABULARY AND FIGURATIVE LANGUAGE

**Prompt 3, Page 50:** Why do you think Part One starts with this proverb: "When elephants fight, it is the grass that suffers"?

**Prompt 7, Page 146:** Explain what a *refugee camp* is.

**Prompt 10, Page 197:** Explain what an *optimist* is and whether or not you'd use that word to describe Kek.

## THEMES AND IDEAS

**Prompt 6, Page 135:** What does the cow represent to Kek?

**Prompt 8, Page 163:** Think about the last three chapters. What themes are emerging?

**Prompt 13, Page 249:** What are some themes in this story?

level **W**

# *Freak the Mighty*

by Rodman Philbrick

## PLOT AND SETTING

**Prompt 1, Page 27:** Describe Max's bedroom. What is significant about it?

**Prompt 5, Page 71:** Explain this scene's importance. What might it foreshadow?

**Prompt 8, Page 87:** Why does Mrs. Addison say, "You're going to be okay, Maxwell Kane. I'm sure of it now"?

**Prompt 9, Page 99:** What problems is Max facing?

## CHARACTER

**Prompt 2, Page 33:** How are Freak and Max alike, and how are they different? What are your thoughts about their relationship?

**Prompt 3, Page 44:** What kind of people are Grim and Gram? How do they treat Max?

**Prompt 7, Page 78:** Think about Freak's references to knights and dragons, fair maidens, and quests. What do they say about him and his relationships?

**Prompt 11, Page 121:** What kind of person is Max's father? How is he affecting Max?

**Prompt 12, Page 140:** Max says, "It's growing up that worries me." What does that reveal about him and his relationships?

level W

# *Freak the Mighty*

by Rodman Philbrick

## VOCABULARY AND FIGURATIVE LANGUAGE

**Prompt 4, Page 47:** What does Freak mean by "Dinosaurs had brains the size of peanuts and they ruled the earth for a hundred million years"? What is he implying?

**Prompt 6, Page 71:** What does "Life ain't life" mean?

**Prompt 10, Page 105:** Do you think that Max is a "chip off the old block"?

## THEMES AND IDEAS

**Prompt 13, Page 160:** What are some themes in this book?

**Prompt 14, Page 160:** How are people with special needs presented in this book? What do you think about that?

# Bibliography

## Professional Resources


Abedi, J., C. Hofstetter, and C. Lord. 2004. "Assessment Accommodations for English Language Learners: Implications for Policy-Based Empirical Research." *Review of Educational Research* 74 (1): 1–28.

Ascenzi-Moreno, L. 2018. "Translanguaging and Responsive Assessment Adaptations: Emergent Bilingual Readers Through the Lens of Possibility." *Language Arts* 95 (6): 355–369.

Fountas, I., and G. S. Pinnell. 2015. "Instructional Level Expectations for Reading." www.heinemann.com/fountasandpinnell/handouts/instructionallevelexpectationsforreading.pdf.

———. 2016. *The Fountas & Pinnell Literacy Continuum, Expanded Edition*. Portsmouth, NH: Heinemann.

———. 2016. F&P Text Level Gradient™. www.fountasandpinnell.com/textlevelgradient.

Serravallo, J. 2019. *Complete Comprehension: Nonfiction*. Portsmouth, NH: Heinemann.

———. 2018. *Understanding Texts & Readers: Responsive Comprehension Instruction with Leveled Texts*. Portsmouth, NH: Heinemann

Teachers College Reading and Writing Project. 2017. "Benchmark Reading Levels and Marking Period Assessments, Updated for the 2017–2018 School Year." New York: Teachers College.connect.readingandwritingproject.org/file/download?google_drive_document_id=0B404rJALRaGwU01YYjI4UGNpYTg.

## Children's Literature

Adler, D. A. 1980. *Cam Jansen: The Mystery of the Stolen Diamonds.* New York: Puffin Books.

Applegate, K. 2007. *Home of the Brave.* New York: Square Fish.

Clements, A. 2001. *Jake Drake, Bully Buster.* New York: Atheneum Books for Young Readers.

Coerr, E. 1977. *Sadako and the Thousand Paper Cranes.* New York: Puffin Books.

Curtis, C. P. 1995. *The Watsons Go to Birmingham—1963.* New York: Yearling.

Danziger, P. 1994. *Amber Brown Is Not a Crayon.* New York: Puffin Books.

DiCamillo, K. 2000. *Because of Winn-Dixie.* Somerville, MA: Candlewick.

———. 2001. *The Tiger Rising.* Somerville, MA: Candlewick.

Gantos, J. 1998. *Joey Pigza Swallowed the Key.* New York: Square Fish.

Grimes, N. 2010. *Almost Zero: A Dyamonde Daniel Book.* New York: Puffin Books.

Hesse, K. 1994. *Sable.* New York: Square Fish/Macmillan.

Howe, J. 1996. *Pinky and Rex and the Bully.* New York: Simon Spotlight.

Jacobson, J. 2005. *Andy Shane and the Very Bossy Dolores Starbuckle.* Somerville, MA: Candlewick.

Kvasnosky, L. M. 2006. *Zelda and Ivy: The Runaways.* Somerville, MA: Candlewick.

Lobel, A. 1979. *Days with Frog and Toad.* New York: HarperCollins.

Manes, S. 1982. *Be a Perfect Person in Just Three Days!* New York: Cawallader & Stern.

McDonald, M. 2002. *Judy Moody Saves the World!* Somerville, MA: Candlewick.

Park. L. S. 1999. *SeeSaw Girl.* New York: Sandpiper.

Paterson, K. 1978. *The Great Gilly Hopkins.* New York: HarperCollins.

Pennypacker, S. 2003. *Stuart Goes to School.* New York: Scholastic.

Philbrick, R. 1993. *Freak the Mighty.* New York: Scholastic.

Ryan, P. M. 2004. *Becoming Naomi León.* New York: Scholastic.

Rylant, C. 2012. *Poppleton in Winter.* New York: Houghton Mifflin Harcourt.

Scieszka, J. 1991. *The Time Warp Trio: Knights of the Kitchen Table.* New York: Puffin Books.

Soto, G. 1991. *Taking Sides.* New York: Houghton Mifflin Harcourt.

Spinelli, J. 1996. *Crash.* New York: Yearling.

———. 2002. *Loser.* New York: HarperCollins.

Woodson, J. 1991. *Last Summer with Maizon.* New York: Puffin Books.